BECOMING ...

WHOLE

GWEN MOORE and TODD SERBY

BECOMING ...

WHOLE

GWEN MOORE and TODD SERBY

TEE GEE Publishing Company
P.O. Box 76072
Atlanta, GA 30328

Edited by: BOB OLIVER

ACKNOWLEDGMENTS

To my mother who is still living and learning today at age 39 plus, thank you for teaching me that life is learning and that the desire to know is the key to becoming.

To my children, Jeri and Hal, thank you for always playing, learning and becoming with me. You are perfect playmates!

To Mary, thank you for your constant assistance and encouragement.

Gwen

I want to thank my parents and Lynn and Lee for all their support. Thank you, Gwen, for leading me down the wandering path of games.

Todd

To
Dr. David Mosher
Dr. Edna Copeland
Thank you for making this book possible by believing in us. Fantasies do become realities.

To
B. B. Walton
Thank you for editing for the editor.

To
Harriette, Jeri and Jace
Thank you for playing and working with us.

To
Mike Gillespie
Thank you for your time and expertise so graciously given.

To Tom and Hal at TMS
Thank you for knowing that the impossible is always possible.

Love, Gwen and Todd

DEDICATION

This book is joyfully dedicated to our strongest supporters, the students at Northside Learning Laboratory. Our special thanks to each for keeping the fun alive in us. We thank you for your comments, your questions, your smiles, your teasing, your awe, your encouragement and your love...your unconditional love!

TABLE OF CONTENTS

Page

STAIRWAY OF LEARNING

The idea of learning is instilled in the mind of a child. This one idea is the most important of all learning because the desire to know, to learn, to investigate and to dream is our incentive for learning! As a young child I went to school to learn. The thought of "not learning" never entered my mind nor the minds of my parents. Until age five, I learned at home. I was taught that school was "the place" for untold learning. My feelings told me that learning was mysterious, mystical, and marvelous! These ideas were instilled in my mind by my parents.

In conversation, my parents would often say things like; "When you start to school, Gwen...", "When you are in first grade, Gwen, you can...", "It will soon be time for you to go to school and learn..." These constant reminders were mine to dream about and to plan for, everyday -- twenty four hours a day. I lived each moment knowing greater learning was to be mine. It was a delightful revelation to know as a young child that infinite learning awaited me...just around the corner in that little country "schoolhouse"!

Born in the country, in a small community in Randolph county, Alabama, I was born to learn. We were wealthy in my mind. If anyone had more than we did, I was certainly unaware of it. All of my needs were well met and all of my dreams were future possibilities. I have no memories of thinking about what others had; I only knew that I had more than enough. I also knew that my future had wonderful things in store for me! I knew that I was learning every day!

The only comparisons that I remember making were those within our family. This included my mother, father and one brother who was four years my senior. My brother was very bright . Following him through school and having

1

the same teachers year after year constituted a full-time job for me. I knew without a doubt that I wanted to learn everything that he knew and more! The teachers wanted me in their classes and I was eager to be there. But...I often felt it when they realized that I was not as quick minded as he. I also felt it when they began to realize that my mouth was never closed, my body was never motionless, and my desire to "catch up with...and be as smart as" my brother, never ended. The following incident gives a perfect example...

Setting: First grade classroom.

An upper grade student came into our room to bring a message to my teacher, Mrs. Landers. Being the usual busybody that I was, I was waving, speaking and running to the desk to see if I could possibly nose in enough to discover the reason for the visit. When the student left, Mrs. Landers came over to me and said, "Gwen, some day I hope you get serious and become like your brother. When he was in first grade, he was always so busy reading and working that he never noticed when an outsider came into our room."

Needless to say I was crushed! I sulked and pouted for the rest of the day and went home from school feeling very put down. After much thought, I made a new resolution to never see anyone who came into our classroom again...at least I would never let Mrs. Landers know if I did.

A few days later when another visitor came in to see her I remembered my "self-imposed resolution". I sat quietly, peeped just a little, and remained in my seat staring intently at my book until I heard the door close and knew that the coast was clear. With much excitement I went straight to the teacher's desk and said, "Mrs. Landers, who was the visitor who just came in the room?! She looked at me slightly puzzled as I continued, "I was so busy reading, I did not even notice."

You can imagine the rest; her entire lecture described my seeking her approval. I fully understood that I had lost any chance for an A in conduct before she finished with me. A's were fine and I made many...but in conduct? Never! A's were for reading, writing, arithmetic and other subjects -- or so it seemed to me.

Never once during this incident and many others that followed, did it occur to me to give up or to quit. My constant thoughts were, "How do I get better?" or "How do I do it right for everybody?" When I made a mistake, my first desire was to go to my parents or teacher, whoever was in charge of me, and get the punishment over quickly so that I would be free to go on living and learning. Where did all of this come from at such an early age? It came, of course, from positive parents and it also came from positive childhood experiences. Many experiences and many skills and strategies were innocently developed through the numerous games we played.

In addition to farming for a living, we owned and operated the country store in our community -- a place that added much to my learning. Before I was tall enough to get a drink from the Coca-Cola box, I was left to keep the store open when my father went for supplies. Dad would always tell me that I could have a Coke when one of the salesmen came by to get it out of the cooler for me. It was certainly my treat to see a salesman's car coming down the hill...the water in my mouth soon turned into strawberry soda.

Experiences of all kinds were mine and activities and games were a big part of my childhood. As I was born before television, our family played games and listened to the radio. The radio was extremely instrumental in lengthening my attention span. I learned quickly that the announcers and speakers were only going to tell me something once. They did not know the meaning of "repeat". Listening to the radio also aided the development of my auditory skills. My visual, motor and spatial skills fell into working order through games such as Chinese checkers, dominoes, Old Maid, marbles, jacks, hop-scotch, croquet, horseshoes, hide-'n-seek, Red Rover, drop the handkerchief, I Spy, Flying Dutchman, basketball, biking and Tom-Walkers. These -- along with the imaginary games that we developed on our own -- were our mainstay of entertainment and skill development.

Other activities that were a constant part of this skill development process included coloring, drawing, cutting paper dolls from magazines and catalogs, (thank you, Mr. Sears and Mr. Roebuck), and pasting them to cardboard with flour paste created in the kitchen. Finally there was the gluing of a stand on the back of each so they could stand...or lean. Making playthings -- from paper dolls to Tom-Walkers; (now called stilts) -- were activities that we looked forward to daily. We even took oil cans and wire and made a shorter type of apparatus for walking. We also made wire racks from coat hangers and pushed and guided ring-wheels. These adventures certainly aided me in achieving balance...of many types. Another exciting activity was climbing trees and building swings in them with ropes, chains, tires and boards. Our balance, fine motor skills, gross motor, visual skills and auditory skills were well developed at home. If these experiences left any gaps in my skill development, picking cotton, thinning corn and helping to prepare vegetables for cooking certainly filled the voids. Shelling peas and snapping beans did a lot for the muscles of my writing fingers!

Living on the farm, chores became an automatic part of my life, and I grew up with a deep appreciation for work. I remember working hard to do my chores well so that I could play. The best part of play was the family games we played in the evenings by the fire and the outside games that we played on Sunday afternoons. It never occurred to me that my parents should not play. They were an active part of my life and their participation added much joy for me.

My mental strategies were numerous from the games and from such activities as embroidering, crocheting, sewing, cooking, baking, playing the piano and later taking voice. All of these gave me a sense of responsibility at a very young age. For example, I recall at age nine playing the piano in church one Sunday morning when the church pianist was absent. There were five songs and I only knew four! The song leader, age fifty or more, graciously agreed to sing the first song over again when I whispered to him that I had played all the songs I knew. Inside, I knew that I would learn more the coming week and avoid that embarrassment again. Making the same mistake twice was never my choice! Another example of this is at age ten, I prepared dinner for guests one day while my mother was away. To her surprise, when she returned that afternoon, our minister and his family were joining us for dinner. Most of all I remember that my dinner was colorful. It included meatloaf, green beans, radishes, tomatoes, peppers and pickles on a relish tray, deviled eggs, corn bread and finally, pink, fluffy marshmallow cookies for dessert! I remember that everyone was impressed and that I felt pride in my accomplishments.

Also, at age eleven, I went to work in a hat shop in the small town to which we had moved when my father became a Methodist Minister. In my eyes we were now living in the city --- my perception may have been slightly off...population six hundred (maybe)! To me making money was wonderful, and I was paid one dollar and fifty cents per day. A year later, the big dry goods store down the street offered me a one dollar raise, and I moved into a new position that soon allowed me to draw commissions on what I sold. Summer blanket sales added much to my bank account!

Responsibility accompanied me as I went away to college. When offered my first teaching job, the thought of my being unprepared did not cross my mind. I left college one quarter to teach for the retiring Superintendent of Schools. This was a marvelous growing experience for me. I returned to college the following quarter with more vim and vigor than ever. After teaching students near my own age and even being asked out by an eighth grader in my class, learning had new meaning for me.

Wherever we lived, whatever we did, I remember most vividly that I was sent to school to learn reading, writing and arithmetic. Anything else that I learned there my parents considered a bonus. The rest of my learning, which included social, emotional, and spiritual skills, was a part of my home life. My parents never expected school to provide the learning for who I was, the values I accepted or the person I was to become. These responsibilities my parents fully accepted.

Today I am grateful for their attitude...I am who I am because of the life I have lived. This beginning provided the experiences that have guided my learning in a positive manner all of my life. I appreciate having the skills for facing reality, learning constantly, thinking...and thinking creatively...and for always being in the process of becoming. The "knowing" that every problem has a solution has been and is today my guiding light.

Thinking is my way of learning and it includes living and experiencing a full, varied, happy, open-ended life. My thinking is based on the analogy of a staircase. The advantages of this are numerous. Learning is omnipresent; I can stand on any step and know that learning is everywhere. It is above me, below me, beside me, around me and most importantly, it is with me and within me now. I can move from place to place and know that learning moves with me. Learning surrounds me wherever I am.

Learning is open-ended, a never-ending process; therefore, my thought is never wasted on phrases such as "it is too late". I have the advantage of knowing that it is never too late; therefore, I feel no despair or anxiety. To know that this is true on every step of my unending stairway is insurance that I cannot fail because there is always more to come. It is knowledge that error is of little value because I have more to learn and am not required to know all that is on any one step. I can expand...dream...work toward anything my heart, mind or soul desires.

Learning is an in-depth process; the idea of mental expansion comes from the very soul of me. Looking backward for a moment, I find a deep, continuous thread that has woven my theme and my dream as I have climbed my stairway. For example, the title of my salutorian address was "Stop and Think". (The valedictorian had A in conduct.) My speech suggested that, as young people, we had the opportunity to plan our learning...our mental growth...and to become... Ten years later, as a graduate student, I wrote a term paper entitled, "The Elasticity of the Brain". This paper explained how thinking forces the brain to stretch and to grow. After another ten years of living, teaching and learning, I opened a learning lab with a partner to prove that children need a place to stop and think, a place to be comfortable while learning occurs.

While on this stairstep I am learning that a parent often experiences feelings of frustration, disappointment and voices a lot of, "I love you, but...", to a child by the time he or she reaches our lab. Feelings directed at the teacher, school, child, and/or self confuse the child who is already stumbling in the learning process. This applies to a six year old who is learning to read, write or spell, or to the eleventh grader whose SAT score needs an additional fifty points to qualify for the college of choice. The student needs time, patience, approval, acceptance and "OK -ness", to repair or to replace a step on his stairway of learning. "OK -ness" is the feeling that everything is okay for this minute, this hour, this day...now is okay.

The child needs to know that errors are only signals to alert one that it is time to regroup and to review alternatives...a time to re-focus learning. The strategies for thinking of these alternatives are available for learning at age ten playing Stratego, at age sixteen playing Inner Circle or at age three playing Tic-Tac-Toe. The point is that strategies for alternative thinking are easily developed through playing games. This is not to say that games always erase every difficult phase of learning in one's life, but it is to say that games do allow experiences for the development of thinking. This is also to say clearly that games provide us with experiences for developing permanent feelings of self worth.

As my stairway continues, I stumble over a step now and then to learn something more clearly. At times I even go down the stairs a few steps to pick up things that I missed on my first climb; knowing what I want this time makes the trip easier. The advantages of having this mental stairway are that learning is omnipresent, open-ended and deeply desired. I do not claim to know where my stairway began or where it will end. I only know that I am deeply appreciative to those who have played the games with me that aided my climb. My love, I send to each as I continue to ascend.

Together we now assist every child in building a mental stairway for thinking, learning, expanding and becoming. The child, in his own time and place, learns that he will forever be in the process of becoming...because learning is instilled in the brain.

THE DEVELOPMENT OF CO-AUTHORS

●

AT THIS POINT "MY BOOK" ENDS AND "OUR BOOK" BEGINS...

●

BECOMING...PLAYMATES

Todd Serby is continuing my climb with me. Playing games alone ends just past dot to dot or solitaire; thus, Todd now becomes my "Partner in Play"! To review the skills of old games and to learn the skills of new ones, we have certainly learned the meaning of the word "Playmates"... (see glossary).

Todd is currently a college student who has spent the past thirteen summers in camp either as a camper or as an instructor. These experiences with children and youth have provided Todd with superior total learning. He is far beyond his years in knowing how children learn...and play.

I have learned much from Todd. I appreciate his intelligence, his abilities, and I respect deeply his *strategies* (see glossary) in playing games. His stairway very often surpasses mine and believe me, I know when I am standing still, moving forward, backward, or being surpassed!

As Todd becomes co-author, I am happy that I have a few skills with which to barter. Thank you, Todd, for allowing me to play games with you. Most of all I appreciate your ability to win so many games yet leave me standing tall on my step of self-worth. Happiness is knowing that through this process we are both continual winners because we are developing new strategies for thinking and learning. Climbing together is certainly more fun than going on alone; thank you for becoming my playmate.

WE INVITE YOU TO JOIN US NOW AS
WE INTRODUCE YOU TO:

I. The games we are playing (Chapter 11).
   A. All ages are invited to play all games; *we* have.
   B. All readers are invited to add their own words for the skills listed at the end of each game; space is provided.
   C. All readers are invited to remain calm, cool, collected and happy while playing; *we* have.

II. The beliefs we share and the ideas that are ours (Chapters 3-12).
   A. In the beginning, Gwen was the teacher and Todd was the learner; Gwen's idea. (see glossary)
   B. At some time, Todd became the teacher and Gwen became the learner; Todd's idea. (see glossary)
   C. You are invited to read the glossary; we wrote it.

III. The idea of having fun while everyone learns.
   A. Please! relax, forget your worries and play; *we* have.
   B. Search...look only for each other's strengths; we have.
   C. Release all fear for self and for each child and grow mentally, physically, and spiritually as you read and play; *we* have.

IV. Become happier...*we* are!

V. Have fun...become *playmates!*

In the following chapters, it is our hope that some of our learnings will bring to you ideas for new thinking, fresh thinking and for becoming... As we think about the skills and the thinking-reasoning processes, we have developed two lists of ideas to share with you. We trust that some of these items will prompt your brain to think of new ideas; new ideas that will assist you in providing new learning experiences for your child. We also trust that these experiences will be positive and fun-filled for you and your family.

GAMES PROVIDE THE SETTING FOR:

- motivation to flourish
- attitude development
- personality growth
- communication expansion
- strategies of thought to bud and grow
- automatic learning
- seeing ourselves as we really are
- being...being whoever we are
- relaxed brain play
- change...to occur
- love...to become unconditional
- permanent growth
- interacting
- mental stimulation
- sampling techniques
- behavioral change
- whole learning
- thinking convergently
- thinking divergently
- decision making
- sharing
- accepting successes, failures
- exploration
- verbal learning
- non-verbal learning
- storing information
- silence to become meaningful
- response to become appropriate
- spontaneity to develop
- solutions to be valued
- theories to be developed
- similarities and differences to be understood
- alertness to awaken
- sensory learning to unfold
- awareness to be stimulated
- feelings to come forward
- attention to lengthen (or shorten according to need)
- learning the value of now
- re-learning
- releasing bad habits, feelings and doubts
- gaining retention
- searching, seeking
- modeling to be internalized
- memory to develop
- maturation

- expectancy to expand
- forgetting that which we need not remember
- remembering that which enhances our being
- dealing with reality
- brain storming
- self-esteem to unfold
- and self-worth to begin to show

WE HAVE LEARNED THAT GAMES:

- help you to know your child
- increase attention
- open the way for communication
- allow you to understand intricacies of how your child responds
- unlock puzzles within the brain for you and your child
- are skill builders
- assist the brain in developing new strategies for learning
- remove fear
- provide fun learning
- add interest to skills
- promote the development of life-long social skills
- assist your child in being honest
- are marvelous in developing values and morals
- improve coordination
- are positive experiences
- activate the mind
- develop assertiveness
- allow attention spans to lengthen
- assist the development of verbal fluency
- develop quantitative concepts
- provide positive practice for fine motor development
- stimulate all aspects of visual learning
- build mental awareness and understanding
- develop organizational skills
- solve problems of lateralization and directionality

- develop spatial abilities
- decrease distractability
- allow growth in receptive and expressive language
- increase reasoning
- develop mental computation
- extend short term memory
- lay the foundation for long term memory
- provide practice in recall and retrieval
- build auditory attention
- give immediate feedback
- provide natural learning
- provide processes for facing and solving problems
- reduce stress
- build strategies for life
- increase speed in thinking
- raise self-esteem
- are healthy
- instill trust
- bring families together
- allow children to learn comfortably

At times -- when engaged in play and absolutely nothing is working for you or for your child as we so glibly suggest it will -- you may want to send us a personal list of your very own...(See glossary). Just remember that nothing is foolproof, but games have a large number of possibilities.

SKILLS--A CHILD'S DEFINITION

Learning skills, study skills, written skills, oral skills,visual skills, auditory skills, motor skills, spatial skills...the list goes on. These are the skills parents desire for their children. Many of these are so automatic for parents that understanding a lack of them in a child is nearly impossible.

A high percentage of youngsters, being right-brained, see the whole so clearly that beginning with small parts to reconstruct a whole is mind-boggling. For example, if a child age fourteen does not read or spell well, he is far too mature for returning to every sound of each letter and reconstructing his complete phonetic system. This was not learned at his appropriate age level, and it will not be learned through the same process now. The only pieces that the right-brained child understands are those pieces nearest the whole. He retains material better if you back up from the whole rather than starting with single pieces in an effort to create a new whole. To learn reading at this age, one needs to begin with reading -- not with sounds of the al- phabet. Many missing parts can be replaced as you are read- ing and soon they begin to interweave and a whole is formed -- from the whole -- not from the single pieces. This same idea often applies to spelling, mathematics and other academic subjects.

Another learning occurs here for parents. If your child has been taught the same thing over and over and has not mastered the learning, stop and think. Something new is needed. Do not allow the same process to continue. If you take the child to a professional for help, listen....listen...lis- ten. Think deeply about each suggestion that you receive.

Working for years with young people has taught us to become the buffer between a child and home at times. When a parent sees so clearly what a child needs, the parent forgets that the child's learning style is probably very different from the parents. Every brain is unique; every brain has its own acceptance pattern for learning; every brain has its own entrance through which new learning may enter. What is appropriate for the parent in learning may never be possible for the child. The idea for parents to learn is to stop pushing the child in one direction; this is harmful for the child. This grinding push lowers self-esteem, brings on feelings of defeat, creates the acceptance of failure and builds a wall between parent and child. A wall far too high to ever climb over again! Doubts become so instilled in the child's brain that, at age fifty, he may still harbor some of them. If parents release the frustration, release the worry, fear and doubt, before these become a part of the child, love is then all that is necessary. Love the child as he is...all else will fall into place. The child then is free to maintain his self-worth, his self-esteem, his-self love, his own value system and his own dreams.

For the above reasons, we are listing and identifying the most prevalent skills. We believe these to be the ones you hear the most. Space is left for you to add others. As our definitions are simple, so are the skills. No child should be expected to know them all. Although each of us has a lifetime in which to collect these skills, some of us have never mastered all of them. Don't ever add to your child's frustration when he has trouble retaining each and every skill. Play games, have fun, do the unexpected, keep the brain awake. Skills will fall into place...the child's place!

The following definitions are written from the child's point of view. Your dictionary may not support all of them...*we* do!

Auditory skills
- auditory reception - what you hear
- auditory association - putting sounds together to make sense

- auditory sequential memory - remembering what you have heard and how you have heard it; things in a row that you hear
- auditory closure - having heard it all; then forgetting about it
- auditory sound blending - getting the whole together
- auditory vocabulary - big words you have heard; little meaning
- auditory word attack - backing up from the whole
- auditory discrimination - deciding which is which; deciding what is what
- auditory perception - knowing what I think from what I have heard; organizing, reproducing and understanding what is heard
- auditory memory - remembering what I have been told

Visual skills
- visual reception - knowing I see what I see
- visual association - seeing more than one thing at the same time; putting together what I see
- visual sequential memory - seeing things in a row and remembering that I saw them
- visual closure - having seen it all; putting it together
- visual grammatic closure - seeing and saying the whole thing
- visual discrimination - deciding which is which; telling things apart
- visual perception - understanding with the eyes what is seen
- visual coordination - putting the whole together
- visual motor memory - remembering and writing what was seen; words "they" think I should know; words with no pictures to visualize
- visual word attack - "going for it"
- visual eye tracking - looking all over, everywhere
- visual eye-hand coordination - putting my finger on my nose with my eyes open

- visual sorting - showing others the pieces of the whole; taking the whole apart, separating pieces
- figure ground - finding lost pictures, numbers in the dirt

Motor skills
- fine motor - wiggling my fingers and toes; pretty writing
- gross motor - walking, running; being the star athlete
- sensory motor - knowing what I feel, see, taste, hear and smell
- agility - moving on -- quickly
- coordination - having "it" together

Directional skills
- right and left - knowing hands and feet; which is going in what direction
- up and down - above and below
- front and behind - here and there
- laterality - left, right, both sides
- directionality - all of the above.

Modality
- modality - whichever way it is coming from or going to; the way I best remember seeing, tasting, touching, feeling or hearing
- cross-modality - coming in one way, going out another; getting "it" together

Attention
- visual attention - seeing; knowing I am seeing, continuing to see; looking at it
- auditory attention - hearing, listening; knowing that I am hearing
- motor attention - keeping still, not moving; knowing that I am moving or not moving and in what direction
- spatial attention - knowing where all of the parts go; into what space they fit to make a whole

Educational skills
- tenses - now; before; soon to be; never
- phonics - funny sounds
- spelling - getting words right
- sentence structure - writing and saying what I mean so that others know that I know it
- arithmetic - adding, subtracting, multiplying and dividing numbers
- prefixes - beginnings
- suffixes - endings
- plurals - multiples
- vocabulary - words
- general information - what I know
- thought process development - how I think
- perceptual consistency - same old thing
- inner language process - the talking in my head
- color discrimination - knowing black is black, white is white
- conceptual development - knowing the pieces are in the whole; knowing the whole has pieces
- logical reasoning - being smart
- numerical discrimination - telling the numbers apart
- expression - whispering, talking, screaming; telling
- differentiating - knowing what everything is; separating shapes, sounds, symbol sequences
- remembering - knowing; knowing what I have seen, heard, tasted, smelled or told
- decoding - taking the whole apart
- encoding - putting it together again
- word attack - hitting every word
- retrieval of information - getting it back and proving it
- sequencing - knowing how it goes; putting it that way
- comprehension - understanding
- perseveration - mumbling and stumbling
- dictionary skills - knowing how to find a word

- mental agility - fast thinking
- manual expression - having to say it
- analysis - thinking it over; deciding what it is
- synthesis - putting it all together; letting others know my decision

Social skills
  - behavior - how I act
  - attitude - the way my face or body acts when words come out
  - winning - pleasing everyone
  - losing - disappointing everyone; feeling sad
  - sharing - giving away part of my stuff
  - patience - waiting...waiting...
  - tolerance - not fussing while waiting
  - interactions - mixing it up with others
  - actions - what I do
  - reactions - what I wish I had not done
  - consequences - what happens after I do something
  - appropriate conversation - saying what everyone wants me to say
  - self-control - not being a motor-mouth; not hitting; not being bad
  - self-esteem - who I am inside; what I think about me; knowing how good I am
  - impulsiveness - doing it now...thinking later
  - compulsiveness - things I just have to do...no matter the consequences
  - social perception - what everybody thinks of everybody else
  - social maturation - growing up; pleasing everyone
  - self-concept - my idea of me
  - stress - too much; no escape

Memory skills
- short term memory - remembering right now
- sequential memory - remembering in order
- long term memory - remembering forever

All of these things added together are a part of me...only I know the whole of me...I am becoming. I am your child...your whole child!

Chapter IV

NATURAL LEARNING DEVELOPS THROUGH GAMES

Often in today's busy world, family members become separated from each other as man becomes separated from nature. This decreases our possibilities for natural learning. When separation creates these voids, it is time to arrange more family activities that give children the feeling of being grounded. Too often children are caught in these distant feelings of separation while desiring closeness with family. It is time to recall John Donne's "No man is an island..." and to remember the need that children have for family oneness. These basic back-to-nature connections provide natural learning because man is an integral part of nature. Man can be studied naturally...man studies naturally...man learns naturally. Playing games is a wonderful way of providing natural learning.

The origin of natural learning goes back to animals in the wild where the young play among themselves and learn from their playing experiences. Playing games with family continues to be a marvelous setting for natural learning. Games are the natural way for improving all learning.

One of the best ways to assist your child in developing his brain to its fullest potential is through playing games. Much time in today's world is spent determining how your child learns. But the glorious revelation that we need to see clearly is *that he learns.* Your child *does* learn and he learns *naturally.*

Children are curious. They are explorers, they are creators, they search for learning! Children need experiences that awaken all of their senses -- including intuition. With every game, just imagine that your child is: learning to think, building his power of concentration, developing mental strategies to which new learning can be attached, experiencing new ideas, modeling adult behaviors and creating a new world of values. These things constitute learning...real learning...natural learning...whole learning.

According to the Swiss psychologist Jean Piaget, children learn through four levels of intellectual development that evolve naturally. Some of the basic concepts in his theory of learning are:

1. Schemes are the way one comes to know an object. To really know the object, one must act upon it -- physically or mentally. Activities of mentally or physically disassembling and reassembling can be transferred from one object to another until the process is a part of a child's life.

2. Assimilation is the active process of taking from the environment the parts needed to develop and maintain schemes. Assimilation accounts for our ability to understand something new. It involves actions that change the environment to meet the needs of the person.

3. Accommodation is the process by which we change our schemes through the assimilation of the elements involved. This includes changing one's self to adjust to one's environment. To clarify this, when you turn down the television in order to answer the phone, it is assimilation. But if you raise your voice to talk over the television you are accommodating.

4. Equilibration is the balance between assimilation and accommodation. It moves the child from his own viewpoint to accepting and dealing with the viewpoint of others.

These four levels of intellectual development occur within the four cognitive stages of natural learning development. The ages that accompany the following stages are approximate, but the sequential order is rigid.

The first stage lasts from birth to around age two and is called the Sensory Motor Stage. During this growth period a child learns through his muscles and senses as he develops certain habits for dealing with external objects and events. Behavior is extremely physical at this time and a child is mainly directed by outside stimuli. Language begins to form, and by the end of this period the child is able to distinguish among animals, activities and things.

The second level carries one from age two to age seven and is called the Pre-Operational Stage. This stage includes growth in physical, social, emotional and cognitive development. Some specifics occurring during this period include strides in language growth, concept development and symbolic understanding. The child begins to relate the outside world to his inner world. Magical explanations also begin to make sense and the child gains a sense of symmetry. The process of trial and error develops, the intuitive approach becomes real, and the visual world affects judgments. Time, days, hours and seasons begin to be understood while space at least equals the size of his neighborhood. The child may continue to have difficulties with some of the concepts of time, causality, measurement, number, quantity and velocity. They will disappear with maturity.

The third level involves Concrete Operations covering the age span of seven to eleven years. During this period a child can: move things around and make them fit, acquire fine motor skills, organize his thinking into a system with inner rules, classify and order, place objects in a series, grasp beginning geographical concepts of space and historical times, and solve physical problems when dealing with concrete objects and events.

The fourth and final level is one of Formal Operations -- age twelve and older. During this stage, abstract thinking develops. The child can state propositions and perform operations on them either by combination or transformation. He can also use abstract thought to arrive at principles underlying actual situations. This period is one of reflective thought as he can think back over and evaluate his own thought processes after completing a task. Piaget believes this to be the stage where a child can "generate and deal with hypotheses about the world." (*Psychology of Learning*).

The development of these stages cannot be forced; the maturation accompanying each stage is a natural process. Parents can provide, arrange, guide and direct the setting or the atmosphere for mental maturity to develop through experiences. Many of these experiences can be provided through games from the sensory stage, where concrete object involvement is needed, to the formal operational stage where concrete or abstract concepts are present.

The influence of Piaget is ever present in learning. Today the generally accepted processes of learning are usually categorized as:

- sensational learning
- perceptual learning
- memory and imagery
- symbolic language (verbal and nonverbal)
- conceptualization.

These five processes of learning are natural occurrences in games. Natural strategies that are sensational develop during play. The different senses are ever present for learning in games. Even believing that certain moves can be made sometimes touches several senses; this is sensational. Perceptual learning develops through understanding the plays one sees and/or performs. This learning often reinforces the sensational learning in the excitement of play. Memory and imagery are constants in the conscious and the subconscious minds of players in every game and symbolic language is always present as game interaction takes place.

Conceptualization occurs when understanding is achieved. At this time, strategies are naturally finding their place in the brain.

Natural learning strategies develop through playing games. Some of these strategies pave the way for abstract reasoning to develop. For example, subjects involving abstract reasoning processes become easier to the child because the ground work on which this reasoning builds has already been established in the brain through games.

For example, in playing Domination, our strategy is developing through moving stacks up and down straight lines; we are adding numbers up and down the lines. This process is just slightly different from the similar process used on a number line. The basic strategy of beginning algebra is placed in the brain while playing Domination -- when a child begins to use positive and negative numbers on number lines of both the x-axis and the y-axis -- and when natural understanding begins to belong to the child.

Comprehension is considered to be a child's ability to use common sense, rational reasoning, judgment and sound decision making processes. And the most constructive practice of this process is found in games. For example, in Time Factor, it doesn't take a child long to comprehend the processes involved in setting up chips for a score. Common sense then brings on the recognition that, as he sets the chips for his own win, he is also setting them for his opponent.

Learning by rote process is another way of placing a foundation of strategies in the brain. It is far more fun to develop strategies by rote while playing games. More sensory input occurs in games -- enhancing the child's ability to retain information.

As parents you have the opportunity to provide your child with an array of experiences that provide all kinds of learning. Through the playing of games, intellectual functioning is developing in the whole brain. These natural experiences allow children, teenagers, and adults to grow socially, emotionally and spiritually.

Social skills provide strong determiners of self-esteem in a person's life. Learning to live, interact and respond to others is a natural, realistic and vital part of a child's life in today's world. Social and emotional growth developed naturally through playing games is learning at its best. Each game provides a superb atmosphere for your child to understand the meaning of cooperation with adults and with both siblings and other children.

By balancing and stabilizing emotions, a child learns to be pleasant and happy. Through interchange in playing games he becomes less fussy, less irritable, less likely to pout, sulk, or throw tantrums. The child replaces these negative behaviors with positive ones which grant him greater self-acceptance. The self-worth of a child is always improving when his behaviors are improving enough for family and peers to notice and accept him more readily.

Adaptability is also a vital part of stabilizing emotional and social growth -- allowing self-esteem to grow. Through games a child becomes more adaptable to others and to his entire environment. Patience, adaptability and transitioning become routine with a child as his temperament adjusts to becoming the real person the child is to be. As parents, it is necessary to learn to accept the person that your child turns out to be. "Loving a child as he is" allows him more opportunity for positive change. He relaxes enough to see himself and to make changes comfortably. He no longer finds it necessary to defend the things that parents are trying to force him to change. The child begins to place his strengths and his weaknesses into proper perspective. Natural learning is achieved through his own abilities.

Mistakes and errors are necessary learning experiences. Learning to accept the idea of making a mistake and knowing that it is all right to make errors often decreases the denial and hints of dishonesty that we see in children. Children learn to accept winning and losing when playing games and soon develop the acceptance of their own skills and abilities as well as those of family and peers. Games are a natural place for children to learn that fair play is wholesome and that placing blame is valueless if not harmful. At this time children develop qualities which attract new or improved friendships.

It is easy to comprehend that as adults we are attracted to people who extend to us courtesy, honesty, fair play and comfortable friendships. Young people have the opportunity through game interaction to gain many of these qualities from their adult role models. They perceive how mom and dad play, tease, accept winning and losing, accept errors, show patience and convey understanding. The setting is restricted enough for in-depth learning to occur... learning so deeply absorbed that better attitudes begin to evolve. Sensitivity becomes balanced and one is more able to accept criticism or errors as they happen. Patience is developing now along with leadership. The child is even beginning to see his own improvement as he becomes less excitable, less impulsive, less compulsive. The child is building self esteem, security, and pride through his ability to respond to others, and to the games, appropriately. The child is gaining balance in all phases of his life...naturally.

The child's natural understanding of others increases as he sees them need:
- time to think,
- to adjust attitudes,
- to become less tense,
- to become more tolerant,

- to follow directions more carefully and to become more attentive.

Seeing all of these in action plus hundreds of other skills occurring simultaneously, the child develops emotionally and socially in a fashion that is almost automatic.

Mental and spiritual growth become automatic also as the youngster develops awareness of self and of others. He learns to: handle stress without exploding, await his turn patiently, respect rules and regulations, and respect the rights of others and of self. Self-worth is becoming a reality.

The child is now happier, better adjusted, more alert, and more aware of the meaning of feelings. He becomes more comfortable with his own feelings through the friendly teasing that occurs in play. He develops more independence. This newly gained independence gives him growth in rational thinking and in personally accepting responsibility for his actions. The child earns his happiness. He sheds such behaviors as self-pity, the need for constant praise, shyness, anxiety, verbal abuse of others, and even physical abuse to siblings. During these weeks, months, years, or whatever period of time it takes, the child is developing self-worth. He is learning to trust his own mind. He is also making better decisions and finishing what he starts. These attributes are acquired through the development of stick-to-i-tive-ness, which is easily learned through playing games.

Other skills and changes that evolve naturally during the play time of games include:
- Imagination and creativity
- The ability to forgive and to accept forgiveness
- Memory, both short-term and long-term
- Better reasoning skills and improved common sense
- Tolerance
- Mood changes are less frequent

Another outstanding skill that enhances your child's life forever is that he is, through playing games, building a base of thought processes on which he can continually add new learning. These mental thought processes are the ultimate example of natural conceptualization. When processes are conceptualized, they become permanent learning. We call these processes strategies for learning. They are strategies for unfolding new information in the brain. Playing games involves the whole brain working constantly and consistently. The brain is the master of all, including the thought and strategy of natural learning.

It is important for your child to learn that his mind is marvelous and unique and that he must always look to himself for the thinking that brings fulfillment. If he can learn at an early age that he is responsible for his own attitudes, beliefs and accomplishments, he can begin to learn the importance of positive thinking, rational reasoning, and self-worth. When these concepts are developed, your child can only have success. Natural, internalized learning has become his reality.

Chapter V

WHAT IS LEARNING?

Learning one thing unlocks understanding for many other things.It is difficult to decide if learning is complex simplicity or simple complexity...either way we know that learning is simply fun when playing either simple or complex games.

Learning is generally accepted as the acquiring of knowledge or skill, especially much knowledge in a special field. In the *Psychology of Learning,* we find learning defined as any relatively permanent change in an organism's behavioral repertoire that occurs as a result of experience. Several other authors tend to agree that, at the heart of learning, we find the acquisition, storage, and retrieval sequencing process. According to the authors of this book, learning is improving mentally, physically, emotionally, academically, spiritually and socially. It is gaining understanding and knowledge plus the mental action that involves thinking, seeing, hearing, tasting, smelling, touching and feeling. It is the process of awakening! Learning is seeking and acquiring inward change that is demonstrated outwardly. Learning is the willingness to consider various alternatives before finally conceptualizing ideas...the openness of the mind. Simply stated, *learning is the totality of our experiences.*

Experience is defined as all that has happened to one in his life to date. We agree because experience not only facilitates learning; experience births learning. *experience is learning.* This includes all experiences whether they are good or bad, productive or non-productive, happy or sad, concrete or abstract. Our awareness of the experiences occurring in our lives determines the depth of our learning.

Experience is a constant in the daily lives of our children whether or not we plan it. The provision of outstanding learning experiences should always be high on a parent's priority list. The brains of children need motivation and stimulation to be receptive to all of the learning to be gained from these experiences. The brains of our children need experiences that force both vertical and lateral thinking. *(New Think,* DeBono). Our educational systems are more adept at promoting vertical thinking which returns to parents the task of providing experiences that develop lateral thinking. Vertical thinking is often compared to the more mechanical thinking of computers -- a child may constantly get hung in one-track thinking, going deeper in a single direction. Lateral thinking allows the child to think of the many possibilities that are available in a certain situation and to produce many new ideas. Lateral thinking allows him to flip the coin and view a totally different possibility. Lateral thinking involves problem-solving. But more than that, it gives you new and fresh ways of dealing with realities and possibilities. New ideas are not always profound, but they far surpass old ideas that are not working. As a parent you have daily opportunities to promote this thinking in your child through the experiences you provide. Playing games often sets up the framework for improved thinking and new experiences.

Learning is thinking and experiencing thought. Since thinking cannot be measured or observed technically, it is purely an inferred process. Millions of new ideas can appear for mental examination during a child's experiences each day. The Office of Educational Research and Improvement (1987) suggests eight pointers for teaching children to think.

1. Comparing, matching, categorizing and finding links between new information and facts already known.
2. Evaluating material critically by questioning its usual/unusualness and determining its reliability by examining the proof.
3. Developing a good systematic approach to problem solving by understanding the problem, designing a plan for

solving it, carrying out the plan and, finally, examining its value.

4. Using guided imagery that includes mental mind pictures, positive self-talk plus talking, seeing, hearing and feeling in order to store this information in long term-memory.

5. Elaborating on material and adding descriptions and inferences to deepen the understanding of material (add feeling to fact).

6. Creating, inventing and pretending allows time for thinking to occur, and to be evaluated and demonstrated.

7. Understanding procedure and methods, and developing expectations for the task at hand.

8. Setting and writing goals to allow faster and better learning for deeper absorption of more information.

Strategies equaling mental framework can be developed through playing games so that children acquire stored information in the brain that relates to all of the new information they approach. Games are important in identifying new and untapped mental processes. Games are subtle because pleasure is the focus; therefore, a child is analyzing facts, solving problems and defending his opinions and decisions without even realizing it. This is thinking; this is experiencing; this is learning...learning at its best!

It is the authors' opinion that thinking and the action taken from the thinking provide learning that is permanent. Thinking may be conscious or subconscious and from the study of psychology we know that thinking involves symbolic processes such as words and images. For example, when more conscious effort is applied to visualization, memory and recall improve to the point that they later become automatic processes of visualization. Thinking translates into learning when it involves one or more of our five senses. Things are learned from sight, sound, touch, taste and smell. Complex learning which is more in-depth is made permanent through a combination of these senses. The senses act as cranks to the brain, igniting the brain in order for learning to be received, stored and made ready for later recall. These facts of learning relate closely to the thinking suggestions previously listed. Thinking and learning are interrelated to the point that "you can't have one without the other".

Learning is necessary for parents if they are to assist each child in developing his brain to its highest potential. Parents must learn that telling is not teaching. This is why we are constantly saying or thinking, "I told you so". Parents also learn that experiencing is learning and that each child must have his own experiences. Patience is the most important part of learning for a parent. It requires waiting for learning. Waiting for thought processes to develop naturally is a difficult task for parents. It requires much patience to provide learning opportunities through games and even more to wait for the child to develop his own strategies. If parents continue too much telling, the fun of playing ,thinking and learning is destroyed for children. It is even possible to handicap a child's learning by forcing your own thought processes on him. For example, when this occurs, independent decision-making skills do not mature adequately. A child, teenager or an adult may continue to rely on the thinking of others for making important decisions. The older a person becomes, the more damaging the deficit is to him. Allow the child to develop his own mental strategies, naturally, and at his own pace.

In playing games you can arouse interest in the minds of children to think of and deal with alternatives. For example, suppose the child is playing checkers and you have his men almost cornered. Give him time to reason...time to develop different strategies for getting out...remove the pressure of "think now". Given time to explore possibilities, the child will develop quicker thinking and improved strategies.

He will learn to use the thinking that is appropriate for each task and for himself...thus gaining the desired result.

Note to the parent: Your brain will expand as you play and your thinking will also improve. Some of the whole learning that you gain may be difficult for ego adjustment. But remember when this occurs, your child is watching you. He is actively forming his system of role-modeling from your reactions or responses. What a thought! It is our hope that you learn the true difference between reacting and responding. (See glossary.)

Chapter VI

THE WHOLE BRAIN

"The human mind is a mystery. To a very large extent it will always be so. We will never get very far until we realize this and give up the delusion that we can know, measure, and control what goes on in children's minds. To know one's own mind is difficult enough. I am, to quite a high degree, an introspective person. For a long time I have been interested in my own thoughts, feelings and motives, eager to know as much as I can of the truth about myself. After many years, I think that at most I may know something about a very small part of what goes on in my own head. How preposterous to imagine that I can know what goes on in someone else's." (*How Children Learn*, John Holt.)

"...people's brains are as different as their faces. Faces have, of course some regularity: the eyes are above the nose, the nose is above the mouth, both are above the jaw. But within this regularity there are wide variations: some faces have large noses, some have small eyes. So it is with the brain. The specific features in the brains are different in different individuals. How the brain develops, how it grows and changes in a person's lifetime, and even how it changes within a day, is an area just beginning to be explored. We may not think for long of "the brain" as exactly the same in all people. Some of the recent discoveries...make that idea impossible." (*The Amazing Brain*, Ornstein and Thompson.)

"When a person experiences something, the entire brain reacts to the stimulation." (*Two Sides of The Brain*, S.J. Sigalowitz.) "Inside your brain fifteen billion interactions are going on right now...thinking, feeling, sensing, caring, comparing, judging, deciding...more than a physical organ The BRAIN is a process...a universe." (*The Brain*, Restak.)

As children grow and develop, learn and understand, discover and respond, unfold and become...the whole brain is expanding. This produces the key to success...the key to happiness...the key to total fulfillment. Currently we are being bombarded with new brain research. "...In California left-brain/right-brain stories are a way of life." Deriving from "the popularly held belief...that the right brain is the place where our creative and synthetic impulses arise...is a further belief that the right brain has been the black sheep of our educational and cultural system and that it is high time it received special attention. Thus the California state legislature is currently entertaining proposals for elementary school curricula that emphasize right/brain learning. Our schools are too cognitively rigid, so the story goes." (*The Social Brain*,M.S. Gazzaniga.) Left brain-right brain has become a popular topic of conversation today. This research provides everyone with reasons, or excuses, for almost everything that one does well or poorly. It is becoming America's new escape mechanism. As we grow in understanding and self-worth the need to excuse ourselves decreases and finally disappears. Developing the whole brain allows this comfortableness of being whoever we are -- to unfold.

This is not to deny any of the research on left and right brain-ness. We agree that "each hemisphere...has its own...private sensations, perceptions, thoughts, and ideas -- all of which are cut from the corresponding experiences in the opposite hemisphere. Each left and right hemisphere has its own private chain of memories and learning experiences that are inaccessible to recall by the other hemisphere. In many respects each disconnected hemisphere appears to have a separate "mind of its own". *(Left Brain-Right Brain*, Springer and Deutsch.)* We also believe that to be a total person, we must never allow our dependency on the right or the left of the brain to subtract from our totality...our total learning...our total being.

The right brain, often having been designated as the lesser half or the minor half, is now coming into its own prominence since specific functions are seemingly "manufactured and produced" there. For example, one of the specialized roles of the right brain is the control of orientation. Damage to the right brain has been known to cause so much disorientation in people that finding their way from place to place within their own homes becomes impossible. The right brain is now becoming an accepted half of the whole brain as God, nature and the universe intended. The left brain has been described as the half of our brain that is most intellectual, taking the pieces and constructing the whole. While this is an outstanding way of learning, research now proves it is not the only way. And even though our world has been geared to this method, we now need to view other processes. The question should never be who is right-brained and who is left-brained. The real question is which side is used most often. Everyone uses both sides of his brain, but each person may be more influenced by one side than the other.

If one only strives to develop one side of the brain, the result is imbalance. More balance in the mental, spiritual, physical and emotional development of a child is the desired result. Common sense demands that we provide children with millions of varied learning experiences. These varied experiences develop each side of the brain to its highest level...thus producing a well balanced child...the child who uses the whole brain. The authors suggest that no concern should have higher priority than providing the fullest opportunity for intellectual development for every child. With this suggestion in mind, when the usual methods of providing such experiences as travel, study, drawing, painting and investigating are not easily put into action for the day or hour at hand; *play games!* Skill development occurs naturally at play...a setting where the "side effects" are all positive!

While reviewing the research on the left and right brain, we found from numerous authors the following information at least to be suggested if not actually proven. We offer this information as food for thought.

Information: The left brain controls short-term memory while the right brain is in charge of dreams, analogies and visualization.

Authors' dilemma: Could our short-term memories ever become our dreams?

Information: Fine motor development is a left brain task while gross motor could possibly be a right brain task along with spatial awareness.

Authors' dilemma: No wonder the left side of the brain keeps talking...its little motor skills want to find a spatial setting for growth. (No wonder it was the cow who jumped over the moon! Did it really take four legs, or did it take two brains?)

Information: The left side of the brain talks while the right side listens.

Authors' dilemma: What does the right side do when it's tired of hearing the left and needs a quiet time?

Information: The left side controls analytical thinking while the right controls creativity.

Authors' dilemma: Is it not sad that the left brain can never create what it analyzes, and the right has nothing analyzed to create? (The chicken and egg story makes a comeback!)

Information: The right side is passive and the left side is active.

Authors' dilemma: How did the passive side become so creative?

Information: The left side gets to the whole, piece by piece, (part to whole) while the right side begins with the whole, (whole to part).

Authors' dilemma: Can the right side go from whole to whole? Is each piece so important when you already have them combined? (No wonder dissecting a pig in biology is distasteful to the right-brainers).

Information: The left has the language of words while the right brain has the language of images.

Authors' dilemma: How does anything get described if the left cannot visualize and the right cannot talk?

Information: The left side evaluates what you are doing...the actor and manipulator, while the right side attends to sounds, tastes, smells, touch and images.

Authors' dilemma: What does the right side smell, taste, touch, hear or image if it does not know "what you are doing"?

Information: The left has control of our normal consciousness while the right controls the receptive consciousness.

Authors' dilemma: How does the left determine norms of consciousness if it never receives anything?

Information: We learn that "boy-brains" develop earlier than "girl-brains" on the right side.

Authors' dilemma: If the boys can hear, smell, taste, touch, see and visualize the whole without the parts and control space, creativity, fantasy and intuition but cannot talk, how do they communicate to the girl-brains who have short-term memory?

Information: The girl-brains develop earlier than the boy-brains on the left side.

Authors' dilemma: Is this why girls talk too much? (The divorce rate is now understandable.)

Authors' conclusion: "You can't have one without the other".
The two sides of the brain are called many different things by various authors. For example, the left is called the leading side, the major hemisphere and the side of the will. The right is called the automatic side, the minor hemisphere and the creative side. This list could go on and on, but the authors' choice is to bring to a halt these comparisons and to work toward developing a whole brain that consists of a leading brain that automatically creates from the will of the major and minor hemispheres...the total brain.

Authors' dilemma: How?

Final conclusion: Begin total brain development through playing games and developing strategies on which total learning continues to attach along the way. Building a solid foundation can ultimately equal success for each brain.

Things to remember:
- Strategies + motivation + self-esteem = successful development of a whole brain.
- Your brain and your child's brain can rearrange its organization for accidents and changes of demands. Although in most people language is in the left hemisphere, people with left-hemisphere damage can be trained to produce language using the right-hemisphere. The right-hemisphere takes on language functions in young children who have suffered severe damage to the left-hemisphere! (*The Amazing Brain*, Ornstein and Thompson).
- The only sure way of having it all is to develop the whole brain!
- The purpose of the brain is to learn. We see and understand according to the way we feel...our brain tells us how we feel. This constitutes our learning.
- Man is a becoming species... continually evolving....the brain makes this known!

WHO SHOULD PLAY GAMES?

All children should be happily involved in playing games with family. The atmosphere for the games should be pleasant and relaxed, giving children happy experiences for memorable learning. When this is true, children will broaden their game-playing base. Soon wanting to share the joy they will invite peers to play, explaining the fun they have been having playing with their family. In fact, as they first venture out, it may only be to invite another person to join the family game process. When this is successful, the child will then be willing to venture further and ask other peers to play. Soon, at "spend-the-nights" or in afternoon visits, games will become a noticeable part of their activity. Children even begin to notice games when out shopping. Or they may see new games advertised and request them for birthdays or other gift occasions. This is as it should be. With each new game, there comes -- packaged inside -- just waiting to be set free -- *New Learning, New Experiences, And New Growth For Your Child And You!*

All children learn from playing games and many learning problems disappear through these enjoyable experiences. For example, poor spellers improve when playing games such as Scrabble, Spill and Spell, Boggle, Big Boggle, Last Word and Up Word. In these games alone, let us examine some of the skills involved. The rote process assists the child in storing the correct spelling of each word by playing the game many times over. Different sensory involvements and different modalities such as saying the word (auditory), placing letters to make the words (motor), and seeing the word put together (visual), provide the child with complex learning. Interacting with others in decision-making processes concerning the correct spelling of a word, or determining whether or not a group of letters is a word, then using the dictionary as proof for the decision rather than arguing, is a blend of social and learning skills. At the same time the child is combining the skills of reception, synthesis, analysis, discrimination, comparison, contrast, similarities, analogies, sequential memory, closure, expression, sound blending, laterality, figure-ground, dictionary skills, vocabulary, comprehension, plus auditory and visual memory and perception. The use of all these skills promotes conceptualizing and total learning. At the end of the game, the child has repeatedly internalized the five phases of learning as he has constantly dealt with sensation, perception, imagery, verbal and nonverbal symbols and conceptualizing.

Still more learning is involved by adding the directions to the game. To internalize the directions, the child reads, listens, explains and produces what he has seen and heard. At the same time he has new experiences in the many skills which promote social and emotional growth. These numerous and exciting experiences add up to the sum total of new mental growth...new total learning and new total brain development.

Do you remember why we first recommended one of the word games? The reason was to have experiences that promote better spelling. But examine now what has occurred in this process -- learning has spiraled in many directions. It is impossible to name all of the skills that are incorporated in the various phases of learning through games because so many of them become automatic processes as they should be. The point is that playing games is a marvelous way to expand a child's thinking capacity. Games involve the development of automatic processes and bring hundreds of skills into a process of action and experience. These experiences transfer to memory...memory transfers to learning...and knowledge is gained. (Besides that, everyone begins to spell better!)

All children should play all games. For example, although a child has difficulty in spelling, he or she stills plays all the word games. If the child does not learn to spell better by playing them, he will learn through experience that it is okay to make errors. Another example is the child who has trouble with mental arithmetic. He can improve his skills of addition and subtraction by playing Dominoes. If his problem is in transposing numbers or matching like ones, Tri-Ominoes is a better game. Yahtzee, Rook, Rummy and numerous other games provide mental math gymnastics. All of these games provide experiences for developing an overall understanding of numbers and remove many children's fears and anxieties.

The child who has difficulty verbalizing still plays Password. As he relaxes and feels less anxious being "put on the spot", his verbalization begins to improve. The time comes when he is able to shift his attention from anxiety about self to the synonyms and definitions to which he needs to attend. Verbalization then becomes more automatic. This ability to attend to the correct process is far easier learned at home playing Password than in stressful school situations. Attention span and concentration are now improving in an automatic fashion while the child's attention is directed at playing the game.

It is obvious by this point that many learning difficulties, which are causing social and emotional maladjustments for the child are easier corrected in games at home than in activities outside the home. Through games, parents will better understand the adjustments the child needs to be making -- because they observe him in the game setting. This improved learning for the parent allows the child a better chance...if his parents do not understand him, who will?

All children learn from games -- as do all adults. And all children need this opportunity. Games provide learning experiences in all phases of child growth and development. Games provide parents with marvelous opportunities for presenting children with experiences that will aid emotional, social, academic and spiritual growth. Give the child time to change and try never to expect too much too soon. The pressure from society is already too intense for many children. In a happy setting, a child more easily learns to handle competition, to adapt to following rules consistently and to accept consequences. These learnings are applicable in problem-solving and they are good techniques to use in other phases of life as well.

In happy play time, games allow chaotic or strained conditions to become tranquil. Parents develop a better understanding of how each child learns and responds. These understandings, learned in simple play, carry over into other areas of life. Games are instrumental in teaching all children to face problems and to work and live through them while they are young. According to Dr. M.S. Peck in *The Road Less Traveled*, "...when we love children, we spend time admiring them and caring for them. We give them our time."

Give your child time. Get to know him through the games you play. Become his playmate for awhile...for a lifetime!

STRATEGIES FOR PERFORMANCE

"Successful students behave in certain ways. They have the right attitude. They are motivated...they pay attention...they are relaxed...they ignore distractions that might interfere with learning. And, when they need help with school work, they know how to get it." This quote, found in a current report by the U.S. Department of Education, suggests that, "You can teach your children strategies for the four steps" that aid a child most in learning to become a better student. Children develop strategies for improving their ability in paying attention, keeping interested in school work, learning, remembering and studying.

With these four ideas in mind, we invite you to look at each one separately and see the ways games can develop them.

1. Paying attention: Games provide marvelous ways for your child to improve his ability to attend. Strategies, to be developed through the thought processes and manual manipulations of games, are the framework on which attention spans expand. Strategies are the fundamental skill that we can develop for the purpose of extending a child's span of attention. Games soon encourage the child to improve because they teach him that paying attention is a big step toward winning. Winning produces a feeling of success. Success and winning in games can be transferred to getting an A, B, or C on the next test in school. For example, a child's thought pattern might be as follows: Paying attention helps me to win. Winning makes me feel good about myself. I am not so bad. Better grades make me feel good about myself. Paying attention can help me achieve better grades and have better feelings about myself.

Another way that games assist learning is that -- during the game -- all pressure is removed from the learning process. For example, the child plays happily over an extended period of time with his family. They play Monopoly, Rummikub or Slumlord while many comfortable strategies develop in his brain. Automatic learning and improved attention begin to work without additional effort.

Another consideration at this point is: "What is the child paying attention to?" or "Is his attention misplaced?" I remember vividly when my fourth grade son came home from school one Friday afternoon and informed me that he did not want to return on Monday. This idea arose because his name was not on the board for completing each of the four sets of math facts before the timer rang. Realizing that he knew these facts at home, I went to the store and purchased Perfection and Super Perfection. He asked a friend over for the night and I generously offered to play new games with them. We raced the "ticker" over and over to see who could place the pieces on the board before the timer went off and the board blew up!

Monday afternoon was a happy time because his name was on the board for having completed all four sets of facts! The difficulty in this case had been that the timer -- a kitchen-type timer -- had held his attention. This is not unusual for a bright child who is a strong auditory learner. The games we played over the weekend finally devalued the timer and allowed attention to be placed on the skills being tested.

At this point, reverse your thinking for a minute and imagine what would have occurred on Monday had this child been punished, lectured, drilled with facts, or further frightened about his performance during the weekend. It is likely that his anxiety would have increased and his performance would have decreased; Monday evening would have been a sad time. It is also safe to assume that good play on the weekend was responsible for the fun we had on Monday evening celebrating his success.

2. Keeping interested in school work: Keeping interested is, in fact, keeping attention applied to the desired learning. There are other ways of stirring interests and maintaining attention that develop through the playing of games. For example, playing word games like Boggle helps the child improve his phonics, his word understanding and his spelling. These new skills give his mind new information for building new strategies that give him more hope for the future. The child is gaining better understanding for his next spelling test, his oral and written vocabulary and his understanding of the English language. Playing Dominoes, Tri-Ominoes, Smath and Cribbage help develop mental math strategies for the retention of numbers and the working and reworking of mathematical situations such as addition and subtraction. These mental math strategies are building blocks for higher mathematical conceptualization in high school and college years.

Another asset gained from playing games for building-interest is that the conversation and interaction during the play creates more family interest in what each member of the family is doing. It leads the child to discuss with his family his school performance. He begins to feel the interest of other family members and shares more. This is a real improvement over his mom's probing about the school day. Many children are turned off by the questions moms ask on the way home from school. Conversations do not need to become interrogations.

3. Learning and remembering: This title is what games are all about. Games trigger our different senses. For example, in a simple game of Old Maid, different senses enter into play. The visual is obvious as in most games, but there is also the pretense of trying to hide the Old Maid and not identifying its position to your opponent. The feeling of excitement arises and brings to mind, "Will you select it?" or "Will your opponent get it?". The feeling of joy soars when you get rid of the Old Maid. And the feeling of "being had" is felt when the game ends and you are still holding the Old Maid.

Strategies of cross-modality are involved here as we consider the expressions and the self-control. The intake of knowing you have the Old Maid is learned visually, but the output of whether you have it or not is shown through facial expressions or other body language. (How is your self-control when you feel caught...can you keep a poker face forever?).

Learning and remembering are treated as equivalents in this book. Remembering is the everyday word that describes our memory system. Memory is stored learning only when we have recall of it; otherwise, it becomes irretrievable -- which equals lost information. Children learn and remember from making things happen, and this brings feelings of joy, pride and success. These feelings can be realized through any game. Games create participation in making things happen.

Children are innovative and they enjoy learning through their own discoveries. Their experiences of discovery penetrate the brain and convey learning of their own making. It is wise to allow children time to think and maneuver on their own. Resentment and inappropriate behavior are often provoked in children as they revolt against being told too much by adults. More joy and self esteem are developed through their own innovations. Young children want to play and they are eager to learn. They enjoy feeling a part of things, sharing the control and getting into the power. Puzzles and simple games need to begin as soon as a child shows interest. Often a tot will begin to play if he sees others playing. Sometimes interest sparks if you just leave things in sight. Examples of these are building blocks, snapping pieces, Lite Brite, lacing cards and other simple things to put together. For older children, the same is true if you leave mazes, puzzles, or Drive ya Nuts within reach. They, too, will pick them up and play!

4. Studying: The one complex term that is used most flippantly with today's children is probably the word "study." Stop and think of the sentences and phrases you see, hear, and feel using the term study. Examples:

- My child will not study.
- She never has studied as I did. (The authors wonder about this.)
- He never cracks a book to study.
- No wonder he's failing, he does not study.
- He hasn't studied since...
- What is studying?
- Do kids study anymore? Mine don't.
- He is always studying at the library, but he never takes his books.
- My child doesn't know how to study.
- Teachers never teach kids how to study.
- My child doesn't learn well because he can't study.
- My child doesn't know what studying is.
- Do you still study by osmosis?
- Studying is the last thing on my child's mind.
- Studying never enters his brain.
- He never thinks of studying.

What are people talking about? What does the word "study" mean to you?

In view of the points above, the definition of study seems to be: Study is the magical ability of a student to organize, analyze and remember everything he has ever heard, seen, tasted, felt, smelled, or experienced either singularly or in combination form AND regurgitate it fluently, calmly and accurately after having added his own superb analyzing and wording that no one has ever heard spoken before in such an eloquent, verbal manner; OR write this information in such a superior way that it elevates his standing with teachers and places him on a pedestal all his own.

Our opinion is that parents need to examine, in total honesty, what they want for their own child and why. We agree that parents should want the best for each child, but the best is different for every child. We agree that it is fair to want the child to be happy, but happiness is never exactly the same for any two people. We agree that you should want your child to be able to communicate, but the question is -- with whom? If the above definition of study is really true of a child, the child would be an oddball, excluded from the normal activities of life, or known as a nerd.

The authors' true definition of study is: Study is the ability of a child to examine, investigate, research, ponder, remember, learn or scrutinize all of the messages that his brain receives and re-sends through his body, mouth, ears, nose and eyes. Study involves the total brain because it is one of the major ways that we send information into the brain for storage. New information and learning fit into and attach upon the mental framework of stored strategies gained through study.

The process of study is easier for the child who is learning to think and build strategies through play. For example, if -- in playing Round Four -- the child learns to visualize his brain as having a section like the board, he can soon see that each little circle is a place for new information to lodge and he can turn the different sections around to fit together in different ways. This could also be visualized for each subject, especially in storing information for tests.

Paying attention, keeping interested, learning and remembering may be the definition of studying. We believe this to be true because a person must focus attention and maintain some quality of interest for learning and memory to converge and store in some treasure trove of the brain.

We believe this can be maximized through our definition of "study".

We also believe that learning and remembering may be defined as paying attention, keeping interested, and studying. We believe that paying attention and holding interest form a new nucleus that unites with studying to deposit chunks of information in our brains which finally culminate in total learning.

All of these four steps of becoming a better student may be interchangeable parts of the whole...the whole brain...or the whole child. This only shifts the truth, it does not change it. As we shift the words around, we realize once again that you "can't have one without the other;" therefore, each is a part of the whole. Each part is strengthened through the strategies rehearsed and recounted in games. It is time to play!

Chapter IX

SOLITAIRE GAMES

Solitaire games offer learning, motivation and entertainment. The mental exercises provided through solitaire games and activities are great for a child. These include model building, painting by number, dot-to-dot drawings, lacing cards, coloring books, manipulative puzzles and three dimensional puzzles. These puzzles are usually made of cardboard, wood, plastic or metal. Even their materials create thinking and provide motivation for the exploration of such materials.

One of the greatest attributes of these activities is the removal of stress and tension. Stress of performing in the presence of others does not have to be dealt with in solitaire games. This enables a child to be himself and to work through the game without harboring the fear of being scrutinized for mistakes. A child in this setting has time to develop his strategies and become comfortable with them before using these same skills in the presence of his family or friends.

Solitaire games have much to offer in terms of skills. Many times they surpass the skill levels for group games. Lengthening the attention span is a natural quality for these solo games. Many children need to move fingers, toes or some body part in order to improve thinking. Although this activity will further develop the child's fine motor skills and coordination, the purpose of the movement is for maintaining concentration and increasing learning. This skill can easily be developed in solitary activities. The same concentration can then be transferred to wiggling a pencil while solving problems and/or answering test questions in school.

Playing solitaire games also brings specific focus to the development of mental agility. For example, these puzzles require both a strategy and a solution. A child must work and re-work continually until he discovers a pattern with which to develop his strategy. Deep thinking and deductive reasoning are strong learning factors in solitaire games. Perseverance is another meaningful skill that is used continually in all of the solitaire puzzles. These skills are quickly incorporated into everyday activities that require all kinds of reasoning. The ability to reason through each step of a task and to reach its completion is often developed through playing solitaire games.

Most of these games go from part to whole. For those of you who are right-brained, be careful -- getting upset is harmful for your health! A strategy is always available, even if it includes finding a friend to come to your rescue.

Solitaire games are our most difficult tasks; we go about one for five on these activities! We must admit though, that we are learning,our performance is improving and we do not give up. (One of these days, we may invent a new one -- one for right-brained people.)

Model building, painting by numbers and coloring are some of the activities that facilitate the development of fine motor skills. In these activities the child is his own creator. A great imagination can be developed through these because they provide learning experiences that every child needs. By working alone, a child learns to entertain himself in a constructive way which adds much to his self esteem. He recognizes his achievement and comprehends his progress toward a more perfect state. Working alone also leads a child in becoming more independent in his thinking and it develops his ability for following directions with skill.

Independent learning strategies help the child to feel more comfortable while doing his homework alone -- without a teacher or a parent. He is further motivated to develop patience and understanding. Soon he will begin to solve problems in homework that are difficult for him to understand, and to do it without getting frustrated and/or accepting defeat.

Models are another solitaire activity that promote constructive learning. Many of the skills from model building become vocational and occupational tools that are useful in day-to-day activities. For example, some of these skills offer a background for organization. Organizing the parts of a model and implementing the steps of building it are effective tools that transfer to any project or endeavor. The road remains open in solitaire activities for a child to become motivated and to develop various skills for future use.

When traveling, different solitaire games and activities are marvelous! The child is entertained and, at the same time, he is developing specific skills such as eye-hand coordination, fine-motor skills and the gradual perfection of his in-depth learning strategies. For example, the skills he is developing may be the ones that allow him to improve his writing and copying abilities when in school. Never underestimate the usefulness of any game or activity that a child is doing. Learning to think alone is reason enough for encouraging a child to play with solitaire games.

Note To The Parent: Following each game description there is a skill's list provided for your use. Each time a game is played, new skills are recognized. Space is available on the list for you to add and/or delete them in Chapter IX and in Chapter XI.

WELCOME TO SOLITAIRE
GAMES...

A WORLD OF INDIVIDUAL FUN AND LEARNING!

BRAINY BLOCKS

Fun for one and all is provided through these little shapes and forms of all colors and sizes that are ready to be placed in all kinds of spatial arrangements. The designs start simple and increase in difficulty. Several different sets are available to make manipulation more enjoyable and more complex. Completing a spatial design involves many skills like visual perception, motor, memory, discrimination and closure. Much sorting and matching is required also to find all of the missing pieces.

There is a good, basic foundation to be found for fractions, geometry and other mathematical concepts in Brainy Blocks. They provide individual pleasure as well as family fun, especially when the pieces of all sets are put together and everyone has a one, two, or three-minute time limit to create his own masterpiece. Watch out, you may become a professional Brainy Block manipulator!

Chapter IX

BRAINY BLOCKS
Skill List

Auditory skills
- auditory reception
- auditory association
- auditory sequential memory
- auditory closure
- auditory manual expression
- auditory sound blending
- auditory vocabulary
- auditory word attack
- auditory discrimination
- auditory perception
- auditory memory

Visual skills
- >visual reception
- >visual association
- >visual sequential memory
- >visual closure
- visual grammatic closure
- >visual discrimination
- >visual perception
- >visual memory
- >visual eye tracking
- >visual eye-hand coordination
- >visual sorting
- >figure ground

Motor skills
- >fine motor
- gross motor
- sensory motor

Directional skills
- >right and left
- >up and down
- >laterality
- >directionality

Modality
- >modality
- >cross modality

Attention
- >visual attention
- >auditory attention
- >motor attention
- >spatial attention

Educational Skills
- tenses
- phonics
- spelling
- sentence structure
- arithmetic
- prefixes
- suffixes
- plurals
- vocabulary
- >general information
- >thought process development
- >perceptual consistency
- inner language process
- >color discrimination
- conceptual development
- >logical reasoning
- numerical discrimination
- expression
- >differentiating
- decoding
- encoding
- word attack
- retrieval of information
- >sequencing
- comprehension
- >perseveration
- dictionary skills
- mental agility
- >analysis
- >synthesis

Social skills
- behavior
- attitude
- winning
- losing
- sharing
- patience
- tolerance
- interactions
- actions
- reactions
- consequences
- appropriate conversation
- self control
- self esteem
- impulsiveness
- communication
- compulsiveness
- social perception
- social maturation
- self concept

Memory skills
- >short term memory
- >sequential memory
- >long term memory

Chapter IX

DIFFERIX

The goal of this activity is to match visually each set of birds, fish, clowns and so forth. This little game attempts to genuinely confuse your "eye-brain" coordination! Pictures are almost identical so very close visual attention is a must. Todd's strategy:

1. Pick one area on the card to place your concentration.

2. Go to the first picture on the master card while holding only one of the smaller cards in your hand.

3. Test that one area on which you have placed your attention against each picture on the master card.

4. If it matches, then test all of the other parts of the picture in your hand to the ones on the board and see which card matches in total.

5. Pick another small card and do "all of the above", again.
    Developing systematic strategies is the vital part of learning in every game. Try the task of writing your own thought processes. See if you can put into words what your strategy really is.

Chapter IX

DIFFERIX
Skill List

Auditory skills
  auditory reception
  auditory association
  auditory sequential
    memory
  auditory closure
  auditory manual ex-
    pression
  auditory sound blend-
    ing
  auditory vocabulary
  auditory word attack
  auditory discrimina-
    tion
  auditory perception
  auditory memory

Visual skills
  >visual reception
  >visual association
  >visual sequential
    memory
  >visual closure
  visual grammatic
    closure
  >visual discrimination
  >visual perception
  >visual memory
  >visual eye tracking
  visual eye-hand coor-
    dination
  visual sorting
  figure ground

Motor skills
  >fine motor
  gross motor
  sensory motor

Directional skills
  >right and left
  >up and down
  >laterality
  >directionality

Modality
  >modality
  cross modality

Attention
  >visual attention
  auditory attention
  >motor attention
  >spatial attention

Educational Skills
  tenses
  phonics
  spelling
  sentence structure
  arithmetic
  prefixes
  suffixes
  plurals
  vocabulary
  >general information
  >thought process
    development
  >perceptual consistency
  inner language process
  >color discrimination
  >conceptual develop-
    ment
  >logical reasoning
  numerical discrimina-
    tion
  expression
  >differentiating
  decoding
  encoding
  word attack
  retrieval of informa-
    tion
  >sequencing
  comprehension
  >perseveration
  dictionary skills
  >mental agility
  >analysis
  synthesis

Social skills
  behavior
  attitude
  winning
  losing
  sharing
  patience
  tolerance
  interactions
  actions
  reactions
  consequences
  appropriate conversa-
    tion
  self control
  self esteem
  impulsiveness
  communication
  compulsiveness
  social perception
  social maturation
  self concept

Memory skills
  >short term memory
  >sequential memory
  >long term memory

DRIVE YA' NUTS

Mixing, matching, twisting and turning these little nuts becomes a game of creating strategies. One after another...searching for one that will solve the puzzle. It is appropriately named! Drive ya' Nuts almost did just that to Todd until his "bright right" created a solution...a new creative, inventive, ingenious solution...drive back to the store (in the snow in the North Georgia mountains) where we purchased it and copy the number arrangement on paper...return to the cabin and solve the puzzle! You see? There is always a strategy that will work! Strategies are for all ages and all brains...when you cannot develop a strategy for solving a problem, just create one! On our slippery ride we realized that it still requires the whole brain to carry out the strategy whether it is developed by the left or created by the right.

Chapter IX

DRIVE YA' NUTS
Skill List

Auditory skills
auditory reception
auditory association
auditory sequential
  memory
auditory closure
auditory manual expression
auditory sound blending
auditory vocabulary
auditory word attack
auditory discrimination
auditory perception
auditory memory

Visual skills
>visual reception
>visual association
>visual sequential
  memory
>visual closure
visual grammatic
  closure
>visual discrimination
>visual perception
>visual memory
>visual eye tracking
>visual eye-hand coordination
>visual sorting
>figure ground

Motor skills
>fine motor
gross motor
sensory motor

Directional skills
>right and left
up and down
laterality
>directionality

Modality
>modality
cross modality

Attention
>visual attention
auditory attention
>motor attention
>spatial attention

Educational Skills
tenses
phonics
spelling
sentence structure
arithmetic
prefixes
suffixes
plurals
vocabulary
>general information
>thought process
  development
>perceptual consistency
inner language process
color discrimination
>conceptual development
>logical reasoning
numerical discrimination
expression
>differentiating
decoding
encoding
word attack
retrieval of information
sequencing
comprehension
>perseveration
dictionary skills
>mental agility
analysis
synthesis

Social skills
behavior
attitude
winning
losing
sharing
patience
tolerance
interactions
actions
reactions
consequences
appropriate conversation
self control
self esteem
impulsiveness
communication
compulsiveness
social perception
social maturation
self concept

Memory skills
>short term memory
>sequential memory
>long term memory

65

Chapter IX

HIGH Q

Wheeee!! High-Q or Low Q, of the two, we are not sure which the title should be! BUT, the fine motor skills and mental strategies necessary to perform this game are invaluable to the learner! Keep one around. Even after one masters it, it is still a marvelous tool for developing memory, recall and retrieval. Many steps are to be remembered if you retain the mastery of this game!

Play it over and over again. It is more than entertaining! High-Q is both fun and learning!

Chapter IX

HIGH Q
Skill List

Auditory skills
 auditory reception
 auditory association
 auditory sequential
  memory
 auditory closure
 auditory manual ex-
  pression
 auditory sound blend-
  ing
 auditory vocabulary
 auditory word attack
 auditory discrimina-
  tion
 auditory perception
 auditory memory

Visual skills
 >visual reception
 >visual association
 >visual sequential
  memory
 visual closure
 visual grammatic
  closure
 >visual discrimination
 >visual perception
 >visual memory
 visual eye tracking
 >visual eye-hand coor-
  dination
 visual sorting
 figure ground

Motor skills
 >fine motor
 gross motor
 sensory motor

Directional skills
 >right and left
 >up and down
 >laterality
 >directionality

Modality
 >modality
 cross modality

Attention
 >visual attention
 auditory attention
 >motor attention
 >spatial attention

Educational Skills
 tenses
 phonics
 spelling
 sentence structure
 arithmetic
 prefixes
 suffixes
 plurals
 vocabulary
 >general information
 >thought process
  development
 >perceptual consistency
 inner language
  process
 color discrimination
 conceptual develop-
  ment
 >logical reasoning
 numerical discrimina-
  tion
 expression
 differentiating
 decoding
 encoding
 word attack
 retrieval of informa-
  tion
 >sequencing
 >comprehension
 >perseveration
 dictionary skills
 >mental agility
 analysis
 synthesis

Social skills
 behavior
 attitude
 winning
 losing
 sharing
 patience
 tolerance
 interactions
 actions
 reactions
 consequences
 appropriate conversa-
  tion
 self control
 self esteem
 impulsiveness
 communication
 compulsiveness
 social perception
 social maturation
 self concept

Memory skills
 >short term memory
 >sequential memory
 >long term memory

LITE BRITE

As a toy, Lite Brite creates just as many skills as any other game . When putting the diagram on the screen eye-hand coordination and fine-motor skills are used. These two skills are used in an even greater capacity in the building of the picture. Putting the pieces on the screen takes fine motor skills, eye-hand coordination, motor attention, spatial attention, visual attention, visual coordination, visual motor memory, visual perception, and visual discrimination. A person must also realize what color goes where. This is done by a key of letters on the diagram that matches a color. This process develops short-term memory, visual sorting, decoding, color discrimination, and visual association. As the picture is completed a person develops visual closure and eye-tracking, seeing that all lines are connected and that the picture has no gaps or omissions. Lite Brite has a person using cross modality as one sees what needs to go where visually, finds what to put there visually, and places the peg there mechanically using motor skills.

LITE BRITE
Skill List

Auditory skills
auditory reception
auditory association
auditory sequential
memory
auditory closure
auditory manual expression
auditory sound blending
auditory vocabulary
auditory word attack
auditory discrimination
auditory perception
auditory memory

Visual skills
>visual reception
>visual association
>visual sequential
memory
>visual closure
visual grammatic
closure
>visual discrimination
>visual perception
>visual memory
>visual eye tracking
>visual eye-hand coordination
>visual sorting
>figure ground

Motor skills
>fine motor
gross motor
>sensory motor

Directional skills
>right and left
>up and down
>laterality
>directionality

Modality
>modality
>cross modality

Attention
>visual attention
auditory attention
>motor attention
>spatial attention

Educational Skills
tenses
phonics
spelling
sentence structure
arithmetic
prefixes
suffixes
plurals
vocabulary
>general information
>thought process
development
>perceptual consistency
inner language process
color discrimination
>conceptual development
>logical reasoning
numerical discrimination
expression
>differentiating
decoding
encoding
word attack
>retrieval of information
>sequencing
comprehension
>perseveration
dictionary skills
>mental agility
analysis
synthesis

Social skills
behavior
attitude
winning
losing
sharing
patience
tolerance
interactions
actions
reactions
consequences
appropriate conversation
self control
self esteem
impulsiveness
communication
compulsiveness
social perception
social maturation
self concept

Memory skills
>short term memory
sequential memory
long term memory

MODEL BUILDING

Building model cars, planes, boats, animals or "whatever" is a great way to spend some time constructively It enables a person to see an end result that looks like the picture on the box. By using all of the techniques of building, many skills that are useful for all ages are developed. In actually putting the pieces together, a person uses his visual perception and association skills consistently. Sorting and discrimination are needed in reading the directions and figuring out what pieces go where and how to place them there. The directions assist a person in using a great deal of spatial attention when carrying out the instructions. In the actual building of a model, motor attention along with eye-hand coordination, visual attention, visual perception, directionality, and eye tracking are very important. Special skills are developed through the sensitiveness of gluing the fragile pieces together. Coordination is certainaly improved even after one model is made. It forces a person to have some patience and to take his time in creating something new. It also makes a person reach for a goal, and with the completion of the model, have something that he has worked on as a finished product. This creates self-confidence and pride in his workmanship. In some cases, a small child may take a little longer. All he needs is encouragement and a little reassurance that he is doing fine. Let him do the work and be proud of what he is creating. He will learn to organize all of the parts, which is very useful in day-to-day chores, games and activities.

Chapter IX

MODEL BUILDING
Skill List

Auditory skills
auditory reception
auditory association
auditory sequential
  memory
auditory closure
auditory manual ex-
  pression
auditory sound blend-
  ing
auditory vocabulary
auditory word attack
auditory discrimina-
  tion
auditory perception
auditory memory

Visual skills
>visual reception
>visual association
>visual sequential
  memory
>visual closure
>visual grammatic
  closure
>visual discrimination
>visual perception
>visual memory
>visual eye tracking
>visual eye-hand coor-
  dination
>visual sorting
>figure ground

Motor skills
>fine motor
gross motor
sensory motor

Directional skills
>right and left
>up and down
>laterality
>directionality

Modality
>modality
>cross modality

Attention
>visual attention
  auditory attention
>motor attention
>spatial attention

Educational Skills
tenses
phonics
spelling
sentence structure
arithmetic
prefixes
suffixes
plurals
vocabulary
>general information
>thought process
  development
>perceptual consistency
>inner language process
  color discrimination
>conceptual develop-
  ment
>logical reasoning
  numerical discrimina-
  tion
  expression
>differentiating
  decoding
  encoding
  word attack
>retrieval of informa-
  tion
  sequencing
>comprehension
>perseveration
  dictionary skills
>mental agility
>analysis
>synthesis

Social skills
behavior
attitude
winning
losing
sharing
patience
tolerance
interactions
actions
reactions
consequences
appropriate conversa-
  tion
self control
self esteem
impulsiveness
communication
compulsiveness
social perception
social maturation
self concept

Memory skills
>short term memory
>sequential memory
>long term memory

PERFECTION

The skills for perfection might be better named as fine-fast motor skills, speedy eye-hand coordination or rapid cross modality. This game is a race against the loud ticking clock which offers its own distraction for the game. It is also a race against your own skills. Perfection requires your attention in the visual, spatial and motor areas of learning. Perfection also requires steady nerves to handle the feeling of being "put on the spot" as the clock ticks your time away. A sense of relief is felt when all the pieces are put into place before the board throws the pieces into the air like flying saucers.

Chapter IX

PERFECTION
Skill List

Auditory skills
>auditory reception
auditory association
auditory sequential
 memory
auditory closure
auditory manual ex-
 pression
>auditory sound blend-
 ing
auditory vocabulary
auditory word attack
auditory discrimination
auditory perception
auditory memory

Visual skills
>visual reception
>visual association
visual sequential
 memory
>visual closure
visual grammatic
 closure
>visual discrimination
>visual perception
>visual memory
>visual eye tracking
>visual eye-hand coor-
 dination
>visual sorting
figure ground

Motor skills
>fine motor
gross motor
sensory motor

Directional skills
right and left
up and down
laterality
>directionality

Modality
>modality
>cross modality

Attention
>visual attention
auditory attention
>motor attention
>spatial attention

Educational Skills
tenses
phonics
spelling
sentence structure
arithmetic
prefixes
suffixes
plurals
vocabulary
>general information
>thought process
 development
>perceptual consistency
inner language process
>color discrimination
conceptual develop-
 ment
>logical reasoning
numerical discrimina-
 tion
expression
>differentiating
decoding
encoding
word attack
>retrieval of informa-
 tion
sequencing
comprehension
>perseveration
dictionary skills
>mental agility
>analysis
synthesis

Social skills
behavior
attitude
winning
losing
sharing
patience
tolerance
interactions
actions
reactions
consequences
appropriate conversa-
 tion
self control
self esteem
impulsiveness
communication
compulsiveness
social perception
social maturation
self concept

Memory skills
>short term memory
sequential memory
>long term memory

73

PICTURE HALVES

This game can be played by one or more. The visual skills of matching, sorting, assimilating and perception blend nicely with the motor skills of interlocking the halves of a picture to form a whole. It is difficult and confusing to see two halves without a possible interlock. This adds a marvelous place for directionality, laterality, spatial and motor development to occur. Sounds easy? Do not be fooled! Pick up the deck and see how quickly you are able to match the pairs and interlock the sets.

Chapter IX

PICTURE HALVES
Skill List

Auditory skills
>auditory reception
>auditory association
auditory sequential
memory
auditory closure
auditory manual expression
auditory sound blending
auditory vocabulary
auditory word attack
auditory discrimination
auditory perception
>auditory memory

Visual skills
>visual reception
>visual association
>visual sequential memory
>visual closure
>visual grammatic closure
>visual discrimination
>visual perception
>visual memory
>visual eye tracking
>visual eye-hand coordination
>visual sorting
figure ground

Motor skills
>fine motor
gross motor
>sensory motor

Directional skills
>right and left
>up and down
>laterality
>directionality

Modality
>modality
>cross modality

Attention
>visual attention
auditory attention
>motor attention
>spatial attention

Educational Skills
tenses
phonics
spelling
sentence structure
arithmetic
prefixes
suffixes
plurals
vocabulary
>general information
>thought process development
>perceptual consistency
inner language process
>color discrimination
>conceptual development
>logical reasoning
numerical discrimination
expression
>differentiating
decoding
encoding
word attack
>retrieval of information
sequencing
comprehension
>perseveration
dictionary skills
>mental agility
analysis
synthesis

Social skills
behavior
attitude
winning
losing
sharing
patience
tolerance
interactions
actions
reactions
consequences
appropriate conversation
self control
self esteem
impulsiveness
communication
compulsiveness
social perception
social maturation
self concept

Memory skills
>short term memory
sequential memory
>long term memory

QUINTETS

These forty-four card halves each have a sum of dots that is not divisible by five. The object is to create a new interlocking set that provides a sum that is divisible by five. Need we say more? This is a marvelous, superb, outstanding game for mental math combinations. Visual perception is combined with fine motor, eye-hand coordination, spatial and directional skills to provide good learning. One or more can play.

QUINTETS
Skill List

Auditory skills
  auditory reception
  auditory association
  auditory sequential
    memory
  auditory closure
  auditory manual ex-
    pression
  auditory sound blend-
    ing
  auditory vocabulary
  auditory word attack
  auditory discrimina-
    tion
  auditory perception
  auditory memory

Visual skills
>visual reception
  visual association
>visual sequential
    memory
  visual closure
  visual grammatic
    closure
>visual discrimination
>visual perception
>visual memory
  visual eye tracking
>visual eye-hand coor-
    dination
  visual sorting
  figure ground

Motor skills
>fine motor
  gross motor
  sensory motor

Directional skills
>right and left
>up and down
>laterality
>directionality

Modality
>modality
>cross modality

Attention
>visual attention
  auditory attention
>motor attention
>spatial attention

Educational Skills
  tenses
  phonics
  spelling
  sentence structure
  arithmetic
  prefixes
  suffixes
  plurals
  vocabulary
>general information
>thought process
    development
>perceptual consistency
  inner language process
>color discrimination
>conceptual develop-
    ment
>logical reasoning
  numerical discrimina-
    tion
  expression
>differentiating
  decoding
  encoding
  word attack
>retrieval of informa-
    tion
  sequencing
>comprehension
>perseveration
  dictionary skills
  mental agility
  analysis
  synthesis

Social skills
  behavior
  attitude
  winning
  losing
  sharing
  patience
  tolerance
  interactions
  actions
  reactions
  consequences
  appropriate conversa-
    tion
  self control
  self esteem
  impulsiveness
  cmmunication
  compulsiveness
  social perception
  social maturation
  self concept

Memory skills
>short term memory
>sequential memory
>long term memory

RUBIK'S MAGIC

"Rubik's magic"?? This is exactly what it says on the package!

Magic? In the movement of flip, fold and open? Flip has multiple meanings. In fact, it has the unanimous approval of your authors to run wild with all of its many definitions. Here are some of our examples.

- Flip, would you like to play?
- Oh! flip, I missed again!
- I am ready to flip out of this situation!
- No, no Gwen, do not get flip with me!
- I am ready for a nip of flip!
- Todd, are you turning flips?
- I believe Todd's lid is ready to flip!
- Gwen's already has as you can see in the sentence above.
- I saw him flip. Ooops!
- Don't shoot that flip!
- Are you ready for our flip side?
- We are flipping to OPEN, for our next excursion with meanings.
- Open spaces, that's our dream.
- Open up, I am in the dark.
- Let's get this Rubik's out in the open.
- How did you open it?
- The possibilities are open ended.
- Is the "Ru" in Rubik's an open syllable?
- The toy store is still open, let's trade these circles!
- Flip it open, it is time to play!

Chapter IX

RUBIK'S MAGIC
Skill List

Auditory skills
auditory reception
auditory association
auditory sequential
memory
auditory closure
auditory manual ex-
pression
auditory sound blend-
ing
auditory vocabulary
auditory word attack
auditory discrimina-
tion
auditory perception
auditory memory

Visual skills
>visual reception
>visual association
>visual sequential
memory
>visual closure
visual grammatic
closure
>visual discrimination
>visual perception
>visual memory
visual eye tracking
>visual eye-hand coor-
dination
visual sorting
>figure ground

Motor skills
>fine motor
gross motor
>sensory motor

Directional skills
right and left
>up and down
>laterality
>directionality

Modality
>modality
>cross modality

Attention
>visual attention
auditory attention
>motor attention
>spatial attention

Educational Skills
tenses
phonics
spelling
sentence structure
arithmetic
prefixes
suffixes
plurals
vocabulary
>general information
>thought process
development
>perceptual consistency
inner language process
>color discrimination
>conceptual develop-
ment
logical reasoning
numerical discrimina-
tion
expression
>differentiating
decoding
encoding
word attack
retrieval of informa-
tion
>sequencing
comprehension
>perseveration
dictionary skills
>mental agility
analysis
synthesis

Social skills
behavior
attitude
winning
losing
sharing
patience
tolerance
interactions
actions
reactions
consequences
appropriate conversa-
tion
self control
self esteem
impulsiveness
communication
compulsiveness
social perception
social maturation
self concept

Memory skills
>short term memory
>sequential memory
>long term memory

Chapter IX

SUPER PERFECTION

If you think Perfection is a difficult task you will be shocked to see what "super" means. Super Perfection offers you the opportunity of using every visual, fine motor, spatial and directional skill that you have in eye-hand-mind coordination! The stress of the timer adds to your confusion as you fumble around trying to manipulate the different sizes, shapes and colors into specific spaces! Your cross-modality may even "criss cross" before the buzzer announces your final win...or loss!

Chapter IX

SUPER PERFECTION
Skill List

Auditory skills
>auditory reception
  auditory association
  auditory sequential
    memory
  auditory closure
  auditory manual ex-
    pression
  auditory sound blend-
    ing
  auditory vocabulary
  auditory word attack
  auditory discrimina-
    tion
>auditory perception
>auditory memory

Visual skills
>visual reception
>visual association
  visual sequential
    memory
>visual closure
  visual grammatic
    closure
>visual discrimination
>visual perception
>visual memory
>visual eye tracking
>visual eye-hand coor-
    dination
>visual sorting
>figure ground

Motor skills
>fine motor
  gross motor
>sensory motor

Directional skills
>right and left
>up and down
>laterality
>directionality

Modality
>modality
>cross modality

Attention
>visual attention
  auditory attention
>motor attention
>spatial attention

Educational Skills
  tenses
  phonics
  spelling
  sentence structure
  arithmetic
  prefixes
  suffixes
  plurals
  vocabulary
>general information
>thought process
  development
>perceptual consistency
  inner language process
  color discrimination
>conceptual develop-
  ment
>logical reasoning
  numerical discrimina-
    tion
  expression
>differentiating
  decoding
  encoding
  word attack
>retrieval of informa-
  tion
>sequencing
>comprehension
>perseveration
  dictionary skills
>mental agility
>analysis
  synthesis

Social skills
  behavior
  attitude
  winning
  losing
  sharing
  patience
  tolerance
  interactions
  actions
  reactions
  consequences
  appropriate conversa-
    tion
  self control
  self esteem
  impulsiveness
  communication
  compulsiveness
  social perception
  social maturation
  self concept

Memory skills
>short term memory
>sequential memory
>long term memory

THINK TAC TOE

This little baby should have been named. "Think What?" We are still in progress in solving this one but Gwen and Todd are improving. We can now get all the pieces back in the box! Patience and perseverance are present; Skills are being checked off of a new and longer list; results will be published in our next book.

Chapter IX

THINK TAC TOE
Skill List

Auditory skills
auditory reception
auditory association
auditory sequential
  memory
auditory closure
auditory manual ex-
  pression
auditory sound blend-
  ing
auditory vocabulary
auditory word attack
auditory discrimina-
  tion
auditory perception
auditory memory

Visual skills
>visual reception
>visual association
visual sequential
  memory
>visual closure
visual grammatic
  closure
>visual discrimination
>visual perception
>visual memory
>visual eye tracking
visual eye-hand coor-
  dination
>visual sorting
>figure ground

Motor skills
>fine motor
gross motor
>sensory motor

Directional skills
>right and left
>up and down
>laterality
>directionality

Modality
>modality
>cross modality

Attention
>visual attention
  auditory attention
>motor attention
>spatial attention

Educational Skills
>tenses
  phonics
  spelling
  sentence structure
  arithmetic
  prefixes
  suffixes
  plurals
  vocabulary
>general information
>thought process
  development
>perceptual consistency
>inner language process
  color discrimination
>conceptual develop-
  ment
>logical reasoning
  numerical discrimina-
  tion
  expression
>differentiating
  decoding
  encoding
  word attack
>retrieval of informa-
  tion
>sequencing
>comprehension
  perseveration
  dictionary skills
>mental agility
  analysis
>synthesis

Social skills
behavior
attitude
winning
losing
sharing
patience
tolerance
interactions
actions
reactions
consequences
appropriate conversa-
  tion
self control
self esteem
impulsiveness
communication
compulsiveness
social perception
social maturation
self concept

Memory skills
>short term memory
>sequential memory
>long term memory

THE SOLITAIRE DILEMNA

We have been playing...every day and every night.
We have found strategies...about which we now write.
We have worked our brains...both the left and the right.
The whole to be the winner...that was our total plight.

Everything was working well...we almost had it made.
Until old solitaire appeared...and began our subtle fade.
Cards, we could handle...still feeling quite sedate.
Jigsaws take lots of time...so speed became our mate.

Wooden puzzles, Rubiks rings...upset us just a tad.
But Drive ya' Nuts and Think-Tac-Toe...drove us near to mad.
Wooden puzzle pieces...were looking pretty sad,
Until some help arrived...thank you, Adam's dad.

All these puzzle things...piling high in stacks galore,
Box them up, we could...return them to the store.
Gone away forever...we would play no more.
Quitters we were not...we knew we had to score.

Strategies was the answer...this we knew for certain.
New ones we would find...and save us from the curtain.
Searching for them always...kept our brains a-hurtin'.
Deadlines were a danger...and we were really flirtin'.

Questions ever rising...Our faces turning red.
Strategies were necessary...to prove what we had said.
"Lefty" kept on repeating...a brain is in your head.
"Righty" fantasized the whole...and...thus the two were wed.

MOTIVATION

What is motivation? From the dictionary we learn that motivation is having motive, incentive, inducement and the result of being incited or impelled. We agree with these but we add interest, alertness, awareness, desire, drive, energy and ummmmph! (see glossary). Motivation is the key to effective learning.

Motivation comes from within...the reasons for its "being" are many! Through our experiences we constantly add motivational ideas to our mind or brain, that alert us to the fact that we are motivated. For example, directions for games are motivation for learning to comprehend. Reading directions and carrying them out is reading comprehension at its best! In fact, reading directions and interpreting them is a mental workout for children and adults! Translating the meaning into action from what you have read is a skill that needs much practice because children need to learn to do this before they develop fear of being unable.

The minute that your child can read well enough, begin giving him simple directions to read. One marvelous way to begin this practice is to buy a game appropriate for his age and reading ability. The first time, read the directions to the child and decide together, step by step, what to do and how to do it. This provides superb practice for auditory skills to develop and the attention span is lengthening at the same time. It begins an interactive process of decision making that also needs to be learned at an early age. It is marvelous to learn to transfer written words into action. Working through this auditory exchange, the child will even begin to pick up on some of the adult strategies that are involved in figuring out what to do. Actually playing the game is a team effort from the very beginning! As the child gains skill in the area of reading, interpreting and planning the actions that match the directions, encourage him to do the reading. This time, you become the listener of the team but joint decisions are still made on how to play the game. The child is always learning in these activities. Each time the emphasis is switching to involve different skills but all of the skills are necessary for thorough learning. Finally, when even more skill belongs to the child, hand him a new game; allow him to read, examine and decipher the rules and regulations ALONE! The feeling of accomplishment and pride that he feels is the key to desiring independent learning...this is motivation that is deeply felt. It will stay with him! It is interesting to note how quickly and easily a child internalizes this learning. Conceptualizing is popping in the brain and strategies are forming and making new connections for additional learning. An example of this quickness comes to mind from a recent tutorial experience. We handed a new game to a child one evening and told him that we would play the game with him, if he figured out the directions and told us how to play. This was a game that we had already spent twenty minutes on and failed to understand parts of the instructions! Jeff accomplished this task in fifteen minutes. He was accurate! When a child is motivated, he learns more easily.

Another interesting thing for parents to note is "Which sibling in the family is motivated to learn these skills." I remember vividly times that my daughter would say that we could not play a certain game if her brother was not home....why? Because he would read the instructions and tell her how to play! Being told allows one to avoid learning while internalizing fear and doubt of being unable to play.

Children need to develop realistic concepts of themselves as learners, neither expecting too much or too little. They discover and apply all learnings to new situations. Interpreting the directions of a game offers a good setting for learning and self worth to occur. Watch for these things within your family to be certain that each child is developing all of these skills.

Directions have a marvelous way of walking right into the brain and finding a permanent home in the good old long term memory! How we remember those games we play! Many senses are involved in this interplay of skills and permanent learning is transpiring! We are playing hundreds of games. Some we play once or twice; others we play many times. Which ones do we remember? ALL OF THEM!! We can never tell you how valuable it is for your child to have these learning experiences through games. Experiences that allow new thought patterns and new strategies to be placed in the brain are an invitation for more learning! Stretching and exercising the brain is vitally important and new learning is permanently stored through interpreting directions and playing games!

Short-term memory is present in every game and it enhances our motivation. The more that we remember, the better we play -- the better we permanently store information. Short-term memory transforms into long term memory and playing games makes this transaction easy! Just imagine how many more ideas you can create after playing games for a while. Storing strategies...through sensory processing...paves the way for new learning. Your child masters all of these processes and you assist this learning by playing games. What fun! Just imagine again... the strategies that reach long-term memory are there forever! The short-term memory can be overloaded at times but this can never happen to the long-term memory. This fact is enough motivation for getting you in line at the toy store now!!

"Each child's memory store is acquired through experience and learning. The uniqueness of each human being is due largely to the memory store, the biological residue from a lifetime of experiences. We will some day understand the genetic basis of the ability of the brain to store memory, but we can never know the actual memories from studying the genes, only from studying the brain." (The Brain, Restak). Learning through experiences is multiplied quickly by playing games. The faster the learning becomes, the quicker the child realizes that he is learning -- the motivation and desire for learning more does truly multiply.

In a recent article in Psychology Today, it is concluded that memory is maintained through a "mental structure" or through a "storehouse of general knowledge to generate answers to very specific questions." In either of these, playing games opens the entrance! Playing games is multi-sensory learning which insures us that our learning is going straight into our storehouse of knowledge! This is storing learning in our mental structure...a structure better developed through the strategies found in games. Motivation is results!

Another skill that aids motivation is speed. Speed promotes desire for learning. The reasons for developing speed are:

- to learn faster
- to learn more
- to give the child a marvelous sense of accomplishment
- to improve retention
- to improve recall
- to add meaning to learning
- to improve decision making
- to build incentive
- to allow the child to reach more goals, promoting more willingness to set new goals
- to leave time for review
- to identify what is working and what is not working for him
- to encourage thinking of new alternatives
- to raise self esteem!

What is motivation? All of the above!

At some point in reading, speed and comprehension cross, at that point, a person has reached his best in both speed and comprehension. This cross-point is different for each person. It is the peak of performance in reading and it should be located and developed for each child.

Motivation is automatic when the brain is busy...busy planning, thinking or doing. Motivation is having the mental energy to do! We believe that mental energy gets our physical energy moving.

According to Joyce Rennolds and Helen Corson in *The Energy Connection*, mental energy "is a little stronger than physical energy and less fragmented." This mental energy gives power to concentration. It is our mind saying, "Get up and go"..."You make your own decisions"..."You can be anything you decide to be"..." You have a choice in becoming..."

Mental energy is stimulated by playing games and by the interaction with others who are playing. The atmosphere for playing games should be positive and happy because children of all ages enjoy games and learning is remembered when it is pleasurable. Games generate positive mental energy and motivation!

Communication is motivation. Loneliness occurs when we fail to make contact with others; we need contact; we need connection; we need to feel a part of the things that are going on around us. When these feelings are not present, loneliness occurs and leads us toward withdrawal...into ourselves...and into problems. Loneliness causes social ineptness and destroys motivation. At this point the feeling of loving others or being loved by them is lost. Life offers little to others if love is not present. "The crippling effects of a loveless life are found in the office of every Psychiatrist filled with children and adults who have no awareness of their worth, no sense of identity." (*Unconditional Love*, John Powell). For children to be motivated, they need to know that they are loved unconditionally. Unconditional love omits all of the "if's, and's, and but's", that are too often attached to love. Love is communication...love is knowing your worth and value...love is motivation for life! "Love cures. It cures those who give it and it cures those who receive it." (Powell). Love is the single factor that encompasses the whole of motivation. Love is Motivation!

Chapter XI

GAMES WE ARE PLAYING

The games that we have played and are continuing to play are many. They are listed in this chapter in alphabetical order. We are omitting age levels because we find them to vary with a child's ability, interest, practice and/or experience. We have also written a brief description about each game so that you will know something about what it consists of before purchasing and/or playing it. Following each description, a list of skills is provided for you to complete at your discretion. We are learning that each time we play a game that we are finding new skills to be added. We realize the same will be true for you. We have left space for you to add skills if they are not listed for you. We also understand that there are many names for the same skill and that some of ours are duplications; you may have your own preference. Feel free to let us know what you call the skill, (see glossary for address).

From our playing experience, we realize the impossibility of writing long descriptions for each of these skills. The book would outweigh the authors! Heavy! For this reason we are including a glossary of definitions for you to peruse.

Another thought of ours was that of listing every game but after visiting the Mart and viewing the displays at the Toy and Game Show, we realized the meaning of the phrase, "continual process" (see glossary). We know that you will understand!

Note To The Parent: Following each game description there is a skill's list provided for your use. Each time a game is played, new skills are recognized. Space is available on the list for you to add or delete. Social skills are left unchecked in order for you to check the one's that are appropriate for your child.

ADVANCE TO BOARDWALK

It is time for a stroll down Boardwalk. The object of this game is to collect the most money by building and buying. "Hotels are on the rise and everyone wants in on the ground floor"!

It is time for you to hook up with your visual, thinking, auditory, motor and spatial skills to do your decision making. Your biggest decision being, "Can you become the richest builder on the Boardwalk?" Have fun building your future! Good luck and sound strategy will do the trick for you.

Chapter XI

ADVANCE TO BOARDWALK
Skill List

Auditory skills
>auditory reception
auditory association
auditory sequential
memory
auditory closure
>auditory manual ex-
pression
auditory sound blend-
ing
auditory vocabulary
auditory word attack
auditory discrimina-
tion
>auditory perception
>auditory memory

Visual skills
>visual reception
>visual association
>visual sequential
memory
visual closure
visual grammatic
closure
>visual discrimination
>visual perception
visual memory
visual eye tracking
>visual eye-hand coor-
dination
>visual sorting
figure ground

Motor skills
>fine motor
gross motor
>sensory motor

Directional skills
right and left
>up and down
>laterality
>directionality

Modality
>modality
>cross modality

Attention
>visual attention
>auditory attention
>motor attention
>spatial attention

Educational Skills
tenses
phonics
spelling
sentence structure
arithmetic
prefixes
suffixes
plurals
vocabulary
>general information
>thought process
development
>perceptual consistency
inner language process
>color discrimination
>conceptual develop-
ment
>logical reasoning
numerical discrimina-
tion
>expression
>differentiating
decoding
encoding
word attack
>retrieval of informa-
tion
>sequencing
>comprehension
>perseveration
dictionary skills
>mental agility
analysis
synthesis

Social skills
behavior
attitude
winning
losing
sharing
patience
tolerance
interactions
actions
reactions
consequences
appropriate conversa-
tion
self control
self esteem
impulsivness
communication
compulsiveness
social perception
social maturation
self concept

Memory skills
>short term memory
>sequential memory
long term memory

Chapter XI

BARGAIN HUNTER

Becoming a smart shopper brings many skills into mental action and reaction. This game is designed to do that. Visual and auditory skills are actually involved along with mathematical concepts. Building strategies and conceptualizing are a big part of your recognizing how to hunt a bargain! Just remember that hunting a bargain doesn't mean that you have to buy it...a bargain is never a bargain unless you have a need for the item.

Chapter XI

BARGAIN HUNTER
Skill List

___

Auditory skills
>auditory reception
auditory association
auditory sequential
memory
auditory closure
>auditory manual ex-
pression
auditory sound blend-
ing
>auditory vocabulary
>auditory word attack
auditory discrimina-
tion
>auditory perception
>auditory memory

Visual skills
>visual reception
visual association
visual sequential
memory
visual closure
visual grammatic
closure
visual discrimination
>visual perception
>visual memory
>visual eye tracking
>visual eye-hand coor-
dination
>visual sorting
>figure ground

Motor skills
>fine motor
gross motor
sensory motor

Directional skills
>right and left
>up and down
>laterality
>directionality

Modality
>modality
cross modality

Attention
>visual attention
>auditory attention
>motor attention
>spatial attention

Educational Skills
tenses
phonics
spelling
sentence structure
arithmetic
prefixes
suffixes
plurals
vocabulary
>general information
>thought process
development
perceptual consistency
>inner language process
color discrimination
>conceptual develop-
ment
>logical reasoning
numerical discrimina-
tion
>expression
differentiating
decoding
encoding
word attack
retrieval of informa-
tion
sequencing
comprehension
perseveration
dictionary skills
mental agility
analysis
synthesis

Social skills
behavior
attitude
winning
losing
sharing
patience
tolerance
interactions
actions
reactions
consequences
appropriate conversa-
tion
self control
self esteem
impulsiveness
communication
compulsiveness
social perception
social maturation
self concept

Memory skills
>short term memory
>sequential memory
>long term memory

BATTLESHIP

Battleship is a complex game of hide and seek. Not only does it involve deductive reasoning, it creates strategies that are used to find the opponent's hiding ships. Important skills such as eye-hand coordination and fine motor skills are readily developed. A wide variety of spatial skills are also involved when looking at the game board and determining what actions to take. Other skills involved in this process are visual sorting, visual attention, spatial attention, visual reception, directionality, laterality and color discrimination. This is also an excellent game for auditory reception, auditory attention, motor attention and cross modality. These are all built and strengthened when oral directions are given, and the player must respond with different actions such as putting pegs in the board and saying "hit" or "miss". Battleship is a wonderful game because it builds a foundation for deductive reasoning. The suspense of what is next and being caught escalates as your opponent gets closer and closer to your boat. Battleship builds trust and honesty with other people, but do not let someone sink your ship!

BATTLESHIP
Skill List

Auditory skills
>auditory reception
>auditory association
>auditory sequential
  memory
>auditory closure
>auditory manual ex-
  pression
>auditory sound blend-
  ing
>auditory vocabulary
>auditory word attack
>auditory discrimination
>auditory perception
>auditory memory

Visual skills
>visual reception
>visual association
>visual sequential
  memory
  visual closure
  visual grammatic
  closure
>visual discrimination
>visual perception
>visual memory
>visual word attack
>visual eye tracking
>visual eye-hand coor-
  dination
>visual sorting
>figure ground

Motor skills
>fine motor
  gross motor
>sensory motor

Directional skills
>right and left
>up and down
>laterality
>directionality

Modality
>modality
>cross modality

Attention
>visual attention
>auditory attention
>motor attention
>spatial attention

Educational Skills
  tenses
  phonics
  spelling
>sentence structure
  arithmetic
  prefixes
  suffixes
  plurals
  vocabulary
>general information
>thought process
  development
>perceptual consistency
>inner language process
>color discrimination
>conceptual develop-
  ment
>logical reasoning
  numerical discrimina-
  tion
>expression
>differentiating
  decoding
  encoding
  word attack
>retrieval of information
>sequencing
>comprehension
>perseveration
  dictionary skills
>mental agility
>analysis
>synthesis

Social skills
  behavior
  attitude
  winning
  losing
  sharing
  patience
  tolerance
  interactions
  actions
  reactions
  consequences
  appropriate conversa-
  tion
  self control
  self esteem
  impulsivity
  communication
  compulsiveness
  social perception
  social maturation
  self concept

Memory skills
>short term memory
>sequential memory
>long term memory

Chapter XI

BIG BOGGLE

Big Boggle is a quick game for mixing and matching your spelling and word attack skills! It works your eyes and brain overtime as your vocabulary increases. It is one of the best at keeping your eyes "agog" as you search for words. Stretch your brain and keep "agoggling" without big "boggling".

Chapter XI

BIG BOGGLE
Skill List

Auditory skills
> auditory reception
>
auditory association
> auditory sequential
memory
>
auditory closure
>
auditory manual ex-
pression
> auditory sound blend-
ing
> auditory vocabulary
> auditory word attack
>
auditory discrimina-
tion
>
auditory perception
> auditory memory

Visual skills
> visal reception
> visual association
> visual sequential
memory
> visual closure
visual grammatic
closure
> visual discrimination
> visual perception
> visual memory
> visual word attack
> visual eye tracking
> visual eye-hand coor-
dination
> visual sorting
> figure ground

Motor skills
> fine motor
gross motor
sensory motor

Directional skills
> right and left
> up and down
> laterality
> directionality

Modality
> modality
> cross modality

Attention
> visual attention
> auditory attention
> motor attention
> spatial attention

Educational Skills
> tenses
> phonics
> spelling
sentence structure
arithmetic
> prefixes
> suffixes
> plurals
> vocabulary
> general information
> thought process
development
> perceptual consistency
> inner language process
color discrimination
conceptual develop-
ment
> logical reasoning
numerical discrimina-
tion
expression
> differentiating
> decoding
> encoding
> word attack
> retrieval of informa-
tion
> sequencing
> comprehension
> perseveration
> dictionary skills
> mental agility
> analysis
> synthesis

Social skills
behavior
attitude
winning
losing
sharing
patience
tolerance
interactions
actions
reactions
consequences
appropriate conversa-
tion
self control
self esteem
impulsiveness
communication
compulsiveness
social perception
social maturation
self concept

Memory skills
> short term memory
> sequential memory
> long term memory

BINGO

Bingo provides excellent practice for sequencing numbers and/or is wonderful for reducing the transpositions of numbers and letters. An example of this would be when child writes 61 as 16. Or, in a telephone number one numeral may be out of sequence when it is written. Bingo also gives marvelous practice in tracking. Cross modality comes into play as you receive information auditorially, see it visually and cover it manually.

Bingo is more fun to play when a surprise goes with it. In family situations, this could be earning a reprieve from a chore, for example. Any reward is fun to receive and funny little things often bring much joy to children or adults.

Chapter XI

BINGO
Skill List

Auditory skills
>auditory reception
 auditory association
 auditory sequential
  memory
 auditory closure
 auditory manual ex-
  pression
 auditory sound blend-
  ing
 auditory vocabulary
 auditory word attack
>auditory discrimina-
 tion
>auditory perception
>auditory memory

Visual skills
>visal reception
 visual association
>visual sequential
  memory
>visual closure
 visual grammatic
  closure
 visual discrimination
>visual perception
>visual memory
>visual eye tracking
>visual eye-hand coor-
  dination
>visual sorting
 figure ground

Motor skills
>fine motor
 gross motor
 sensory motor

Directional skills
>right and left
>up and down
>laterality
>directionality

Modality
>modality
>cross modality

Attention
>visual attention
>auditory attention
>motor attention
>spatial attention

Educational Skills
 tenses
 phonics
 spelling
 sentence structure
 arithmetic
 prefixes
 suffixes
 plurals
>vocabulary
>general information
>thought process
 development
>perceptual consistency
 inner language process
 color discrimination
 conceptual develop-
  ment
 logical reasoning
>numerical discrimina-
 tion
 expression
>differentiating
 decoding
 encoding
 word attack
>retrieval of informa-
 tion
>sequencing
>comprehension
>perseveration
 dictionary skills
>mental agility
 analysis
 synthesis

Social skills
 behavior
 attitude
 winning
 losing
 sharing
 patience
 tolerance
 interactions
 actions
 reactions
 consequences
 appropriate conversa-
  tion
 self control
 self esteem
 impulsiveness
 communication
 compulsiveness
 social perception
 social maturation
 self concept

Memory skills
>short term memory
>sequential memory
>long term memory

BRAIN WAVES

Brain Waves is a unique game for two people. Each player has three different colored pieces to move from one side of the board to the other. During a players's turn, he rolls a die, mentally chooses which man to move, and turns his hidden color knob to the color selected. His opponent also has a hidden knob and tries to set it on the very same color. After both have done this, a button is pushed to see which colors light. A match of the lights means a player is blocked. The first to get two men all the way across the board wins. This gives each player practice in keeping an expressionless face in order to avoid giving the opponent obvious facial clues. A lot of strategy is involved in Brain Waves. Also involved are skills such as visual perception and attention, eye-hand coordination and careful attention in motor movement to prevent the disclosure of your color choice as you turn your knob. A little ESP never hurt the soul!

Chapter XI

BRAIN WAVES
Skill List

Auditory skills
>auditory reception
  auditory association
  auditory sequential
    memory
  auditory closure
>auditory manual ex-
  pression
  auditory sound blend-
    ing
  auditory vocabulary
  auditory word attack
  auditory discrimina-
    tion
  auditory perception
>auditory memory

Visual skills
>visual reception
>visual association
>visual sequential
  memory
  visual closure
  visual grammatic
    closure
>visual discrimination
>visual perception
>visual memory
  visual word attack
>visual eye tracking
>visual eye-hand coor-
  dination
  visual sorting
  figure ground

Motor skills
>fine motor
  gross motor
  sensory motor

Directional skills
>right and left
>up and down
>laterality
>directionality

Modality
>modality
>cross modality

Attention
>visual attention
>auditory attention
>motor attention
>spatial attention

Educational Skills
  tenses
  phonics
  spelling
>sentence structure
  arithmetic
  prefixes
  suffixes
  plurals
  vocabulary
>general information
  thought process
    development
>perceptual consistency
>inner language process
>color discrimination
>conceptual develop-
  ment
>logical reasoning
  numerical discrimina-
    tion
>expression
>differentiating
>decoding
  encoding
  word attack
>retrieval of informa-
  tion
  sequencing
  comprehension
  perseveration
  dictionary skills
  mental agility
  analysis
  synthesis

Social skills
  behavior
  attitude
  winning
  losing
  sharing
  patience
  tolerance
  interactions
  actions
  reactions
  consequences
  appropriate conversa-
    tion
  self control
  self esteem
  impulsivity
  communication
  compulsiveness
  social perception
  social maturation
  self concept
  stress

Memory skills
>short term memory
  sequential memory
  long term memory

BOGGLE

Boggle is a fast moving word game that includes dozens of skills! As fast as you get your eyes searching for new words, your mind is sounding and blending letters and combinations of letters to assist you. All of the visual skills are working at full capacity in this game. Rather than talking, you are writing intensely on your individual word list...hoping that it will be adequate when you compare it to your opponents. Spelling is the final measure of your wisdom. Take it easy, unnecessary errors can be avoided as you Boggle along building tons of new words.

Chapter XI

BOGLE
Skill List

Auditory skills
 auditory reception
 auditory association
>auditory sequential
  memory
 auditory closure
 auditory manual ex-
  pression
>auditory sound blend-
  ing
>auditory vocabulary
>auditory word attack
>auditory discrimina-
  tion
 auditory perception
>auditory memory

Visual skills
>visual reception
>visual association
>visual sequential
  memory
>visual closure
 visual grammatic
  closure
>visual discrimination
>visual perception
>visual memory
>visual eye tracking
>visual eye-hand coor-
  dination
>visual sorting
>figure ground

Motor skills
>fine motor
 gross motor
 sensory motor

Directional skills
>right and left
>up and down
>laterality
>directionality

Modality
>modality
>cross modality

Attention
>visual attention
>auditory attention
>motor attention
>spatial attention

Educational Skills
>tenses
>phonics
>spelling
 sentence structure
 arithmetic
>prefixes
>suffixes
>plurals
>vocabulary
>general information
>thought process
  development
>perceptual consistency
>inner language process
 color discrimination
>conceptual develop-
  ment
>logical reasoning
 numerical discrimina-
  tion
 expression
>differentiating
>decoding
>encoding
>word attack
>retrieval of informa-
  tion
>sequencing
>comprehension
>perseveration
 dictionary skills
>mental agility
>analysis

>synthesis

Social skills
 behavior
 attitude
 winning
 losing
 sharing
 patience
 tolerance
 interactions
 actions
 reactions
 consequences
 appropriate conversa-
  tion
 self control
 self esteem
 impulsiveness
 communication
 compulsiveness
 social perception
 social maturation
 self concept

Memory skills
>short term memory
>sequential memory
>long term memory

Chapter XI

CANDY LAND

Candy Land is a super game for young children. As the child moves his Gingerbread man, many skills are being used. Making one's way past Lord Licorice and Molasses Swamp is fun as well as entertaining. The moving of the gingerbread man goes from color to color on this very colorful board. As you travel through Candy Land, color discrimination, visual matching, visual perception and visual reception are practiced. Accepting the ups and downs in the game begins a child's internalization of adaptability. For instance, one's gingerbread man has only one space left before winning, but it can still be sent back to Mr. Plumpy, Mr. Mint or even old Jolly, just to name a few. Yet everyone continues on until some gingerbread man finds the king and his castle. This game is a lot of fun for little children. It has easy directions that any child can understand. Would you like to visit the castle???

Chapter XI

CANDY LAND
Skill List

Auditory skills
> auditory reception
auditory association
auditory sequential
memory
auditory closure
> auditory manual ex-
pression
auditory sound blend-
ing
auditory vocabulary
> auditory word attack
> auditory discrimina-
tion
> auditory perception
> auditory memory

Visual skills
> visual reception
visual association
visual sequential
memory
visual closure
visual grammatic
closure
> visual discrimination
> visual perception
> visual memory
> visual eye tracking
> visual eye-hand coor-
dination
> visual sorting
> figure ground

Motor skills
fine motor
gross motor
> sensory motor

Directional skills
> right and left
> up and down
> laterality
> directionality

Modality
> modality
> cross modality

Attention
> visual attention
> auditory attention
> motor attention
> spatial attention

Educational Skills
tenses
phonics
spelling
sentence structure
arithmetic
prefixes
suffixes
plurals
vocabulary
> general information
> thought process
development
> perceptual consistency
inner language process
> color discrimination
> conceptual develop-
ment
> logical reasoning
numerical discrimina-
tion
> expression
> differentiating
decoding
encoding
word attack
> retrieval of informa-
tion
> sequencing
> comprehension
> perseveration
dictionary skills
> mental agility
> analysis
synthesis

Social skills
behavior
attitude
winning
losing
sharing
patience
tolerance
interactions
actions
reactions
consequences
appropriate conversa-
tion
self control
self esteem
impulsiveness
communication
compulsiveness
social perception
social maturation
self concept

Memory skills
> short term memory
> sequential memory
long term memory

Chapter XI

CASINO YAHTZEE

This game is marvelous for its emphasis on discrimination! Color discrimination, visual discrimination, numerical discrimination, sorting, sequencing, associating and tracking all interweave into an open and internalized learning of fine differences. Attention is present and accounted for in every play! Cross modality controls much of the mental action that is busy transferring from one area to another. Math skills include mental math, counting, multiplication and addition in scoring; all of these add up to a good game. Directionality and short term memory add to the alertness of each player. We believe that after mastering Yahtzee and Jackpot Yahtzee, it is time for a play at the casino!

CASINO YATZEE
Skill List

Auditory skills
>auditory reception
auditory association
>auditory sequential
memory
auditory closure
>auditory manual expression
auditory sound blending
>auditory vocabulary
auditory word attack
>auditory discrimination
>auditory perception
>auditory memory

Visual skills
>visual reception
>visual association
>visual sequential
memory
visual closure
visual grammatic
closure
>visual discrimination
>visual perception
>visual memory
>visual eye tracking
>visual eye-hand coordination
>visual sorting
figure ground

Motor skills
>fine motor
gross motor
sensory motor

Directional skills
>right and left
up and down
>laterality
>directionality

Modality
>modality
>cross modality

Attention
>visual attention
>auditory attention
>motor attention
>spatial attention

Educational Skills
tenses
phonics
spelling
sentence structure
>arithmetic
prefixes
suffixes
plurals
vocabulary
>general information
>thought process
development
>perceptual consistency
inner language process
color discrimination
>conceptual development
>logical reasoning
>numerical discrimination
>expression
>differentiating
decoding
encoding
word attack
>retrieval of information
>sequencing
>comprehension
>perseveration
dictionary skills
>mental agility
>analysis
>synthesis

Social skills
behavior
attitude
winning
losing
sharing
patience
tolerance
interactions
actions
reactions
consequences
appropriate conversation
self control
self esteem
impulsiveness
communication
compulsiveness
social perception
social maturation
self concept

Memory skills
>short term memory
>sequential memory
>long term memory

CHECKERS

The game of the centuries is certainly holding its own with plenty of skills. Checkers gives us opportunity to develop the fine motor skills of finger-muscle movement and eye-hand coordination. It also brings our attention to the forefront for all motor, visual and spatial activities. Checkers awakens the need for color coordination and visual skills including reception, perception, memory, sorting and discrimination. Directionality actually becomes a part of the games strategy and is involved in every move. Strategy and checkers go together like ice cream and apple pie. They have a togetherness that just cannot be separated.

CHECKERS
Skill List

Auditory skills
>auditory reception
auditory association
auditory sequential
   memory
auditory closure
auditory manual ex-
   pression
auditory sound blend-
   ing
auditory vocabulary
auditory word attack
auditory discrimination
auditory perception
auditory memory

Visual skills
>visual reception
>visual association
visual sequential
   memory
visual closure
visual grammatic
   closure
>visual discrimination
>visual perception
>visual memory
>visual eye tracking
>visual eye-hand coor-
   dination
>visual sorting
figure ground

Motor skills
>fine motor
gross motor
sensory motor

Directional skills
>right and left
>up and down
>laterality
>directionality

Modality
>modality
>cross modality

Attention
>visual attention
auditory attention
>motor attention
>spatial attention

Educational Skills
tenses
phonics
spelling
sentence structure
arithmetic
prefixes
suffixes
plurals
vocabulary
>general information
>thought process
   development
>perceptual consistency
>inner language process
>color discrimination
>conceptual develop-
   ment
>logical reasoning
numerical discrimina-
   tion
expression
>differentiating
decoding
encoding
word attack
>retrieval of informa-
   tion
sequencing
>comprehension
>perseveration
dictionary skills
>mental agility
analysis
>synthesis

Social skills
behavior
attitude
winning
losing
sharing
patience
tolerance
interactions
actions
reactions
consequences
appropriate conversa-
   tion
self control
self esteem
impulsiveness
communication
compulsiveness
social perception
social maturation
self concept

Memory skills
>short term memory
>sequential memory
>long term memory

111

CHESS

There is only one thing to say about Chess; it is higher thinking at its utmost. The skills involved are strong builders of basic strategies for abstract thinking to latch on and hold for permanent learning. A large amount of the time in this game involves one using visual, spatial and motor attention due to watching the moves on the board. Eye tracking, directionality and spatial orientation are all intertwined with short term memory to set your strategy and play the game. The possibilities are endless and tremendous as one begins to develop his skills. The thought processes developed through constructing strategies are enough to provide the player with a sense of pride and accomplishment every time he makes a good play.

CHESS
Skill List

Auditory skills
>auditory reception
auditory association
auditory sequential
memory
auditory closure
>auditory manual ex-
pression
auditory sound blend-
ing
auditory vocabulary
auditory word attack
auditory discrimination
>auditory perception
>auditory memory

Visual skills
>visual reception
visual association
>visual sequential
memory
>visual closure
>visual grammatic
closure
>visual discrimination
>visual perception
>visual memory
>visual eye tracking
>visual eye-hand coor-
dination
>visual sorting
>figure ground

Motor skills
>fine motor
gross motor
>sensory motor

Directional skills
>right and left
>up and down
>laterality
>directionality

Modality
>modality
>cross modality

Attention
>visual attention
>auditory attention
>motor attention
>spatial attention

Educational Skills
tenses
phonics
spelling
sentence structure
arithmetic
prefixes
suffixes
plurals
vocabulary
>general information
>thought process
development
>perceptual consistency
>inner language process
>color discrimination
>conceptual develop-
ment
>logical reasoning
numerical discrimina-
tion
>expression
>differentiating
decoding
encoding
word attack
>retrieval of informa-
tion
>sequencing
>comprehension
>perseveration
dictionary skills
>mental agility
>analysis

>synthesis

Social skills
behavior
attitude
winning
losing
sharing
patience
tolerance
interactions
actions
reactions
consequences
appropriate conversa-
tion
self control
self esteem
impulsiveness
communication
compulsiveness
social perception
social maturation
self concept

Memory skills
>short term memory
>sequential memory
>long term memory

CHINESE CHECKERS

Get all your marbles rolling in the right direction! Build roads, trails, jump around, travel and combine your strategies through motor, spatial and visual attention. Visual reception, perception, discrimination, coordination, tracking and sorting are all in play as you develop your strategies of directionality and reasoning. This game really gives you a visual workout when you have four players, but it is fun for two. This is especially true if one needs to learn to attend to fewer visual tasks before additional ones are added.

We thank the Chinese, not only for sharing their cuisine, but for giving our brains new strategies. Chinese checkers must be international learning at its best!

Chapter XI

CHINESE CHECKERS
Skill List

Auditory skills
>auditory reception
auditory association
auditory sequential memory
auditory closure
auditory manual expression
auditory sound blending
>auditory vocabulary
auditory word attack
auditory discrimination
auditory perception
>auditory memory

Visual skills
>visual reception
>visual association
>visual sequential memory
>visual closure
visual grammatic closure
>visual discrimination
>visual perception
>visual memory
>visual eye tracking
>visual eye-hand coordination
>visual sorting
figure ground

Motor skills
>fine motor
gross motor
>sensory motor

Directional skills
>right and left
>up and down
>laterality
>directionality

Modality
>modality
>cross modality

Attention
>visual attention
>auditory attention
>motor attention
>spatial attention

Educational Skills
tenses
phonics
spelling
sentence structure
arithmetic
prefixes
suffixes
plurals
vocabulary
>general information
>thought process development
>perceptual consistency
inner language process
>color discrimination
>conceptual development
>logical reasoning
numerical discrimination
expression
>differentiating
decoding
encoding
word attack
retrieval of information
>sequencing
comprehension
perseveration
dictionary skills
>mental agility
>analysis
synthesis

Social skills
behavior
attitude
winning
losing
sharing
patience
tolerance
interactions
actions
reactions
consequences
appropriate conversation
self control
self esteem
impulsiveness
communication
compulsiveness
social perception
social maturation
self concept

Memory skills
>short term memory
>sequential memory
>long term memory

115

CHUTES AND LADDERS

The climb to the top is full of ups and downs in Chutes and Ladders, just as it is in real life. As soon as you climb up the ladder it is quite possible to slide right back down the chute. This is a game that is good for children and adults to play because adults can point out why a piece gets to climb the ladder or down the chute. It is a subtle game of values that provides marvelous learning for the young child. The first one reaching the top wins, so do not let your man get his hand caught in the cookie jar. Directionality and counting are incorporated as one spins a number and moves his piece the required number of spaces. Visual perception and discrimination are also touched upon as one watches all of the many pictures and spaces on the board. Oops, here I go down the chute again!

Chapter XI

CHUTES AND LADDERS
Skill List

Auditory skills
>auditory reception
auditory association
auditory sequential
memory
auditory closure
>auditory manual ex-
pression
auditory sound blend-
ing
auditory vocabulary
auditory word attack
auditory discrimina-
tion
auditory perception
>auditory memory

Visual skills
>visual reception
visual association
visual sequential
memory
visual closure
visual grammatic
closure
>visual discrimination
>visual perception
>visual memory
>visual eye tracking
>visual eye-hand coor-
dination
>visual sorting
figure ground

Motor skills
>fine motor
gross motor
sensory motor

Directional skills
>right and left
>up and down
>laterality
>directionality

Modality
>modality
cross modality

Attention
>visual attention
auditory attention
>motor attention
>spatial attention

Educational Skills
tenses
phonics
spelling
sentence structure
arithmetic
prefixes
suffixes
plurals
vocabulary
>general information
>thought process
development
perceptual consistency
inner language process
>color discrimination
>conceptual develop-
ment
logical reasoning
>numerical discrimina-
tion
expression
differentiating
decoding
encoding
word attack
retrieval of informa-
tion
>sequencing
comprehension
perseveration
dictionary skills
mental agility
analysis
synthesis

Social skills
behavior
attitude
winning
losing
sharing
patience
tolerance
interactions
actions
reactions
consequences
appropriate conversa-
tion
self control
self esteem
impulsiveness
communication
compulsiveness
social perception
social maturation
self concept

Memory skills
>short term memory
>sequential memory
>long term memory

117

CLUE

Clue is the perfect game for mystery buffs. The object is simple, just find who committed the murder, where it was committed, and with what object. This game is good for providing more abstract thinking as you analyze the incoming information in your quest for the killer. Both visual and auditory skills are included as the information is asked and the answer is shown. Organization of information is also important because one must organize all of the clues to make an exact guess. Good luck, working your way through the mansion. Remember that the butler is not even in the game.

CLUE
Skill List

Auditory skills
>auditory reception
>auditory association
>auditory sequential
  memory
  auditory closure
>auditory manual ex-
  pression
  auditory sound blend-
  ing
>auditory vocabulary
  auditory word attack
>auditory discrimina-
  tion
>auditory perception
>auditory memory

Visual skills
>visual reception
>visual association
  visual sequential
  memory
  visual closure
  visual grammatic
  closure
>visual discrimination
>visual perception
>visual memory
>visual eye tracking
>visual eye-hand coor-
  dination
>visual sorting
  figure ground

Motor skills
>fine motor
  gross motor
  sensory motor

Directional skills
  right and left
  up and down
  laterality
>directionality

Modality
>modality
  cross modality

Attention
>visual attention
>auditory attention
>motor attention
>spatial attention

Educational Skills
  tenses
  phonics
  spelling
  sentence structure
  arithmetic
  prefixes
  suffixes
  plurals
  vocabulary
>general information
>thought process
  development
  perceptual consistency
  inner language process
  color discrimination
  conceptual develop-
  ment
>logical reasoning
  numerical discrimina-
  tion
  expression
>differentiating
  decoding
  encoding
  word attack
>retrieval of informa-
  tion
  sequencing
>comprehension
  perseveration
  dictionary skills
>mental agility
>analysis
>synthesis

Social skills
  behavior
  attitude
  winning
  losing
  sharing
  patience
  tolerance
  interactions
  actions
  reactions
  consequences
  appropriate conversa-
  tion
  self control
  self esteem
  impulsiveness
  communication
  compulsiveness
  social perception
  social maturation
  self concept

Memory skills
>short term memory
>sequential memory
>long term memory

CONCENTRATION

Concentration is a good game for translating pictures and symbols. Visual, auditory and mental skills work furiously in this game! Good auditory sequencing, sounding and blending play a major role! It is interesting to see how others "thought you would think". Try making a few of these to try on each other. It is a marvelous way of practicing skills that really need to be learned more thoroughly. Cross symbol matching and cross modality plus inference ability from symbolic language are all present in this game of rebuses.

Chapter XI

CONCENTRATION
Skill List

Auditory skills
>auditory reception
>auditory association
>auditory sequential
  memory
>auditory closure
>auditory manual ex-
  pression
>auditory sound blend-
  ing
>auditory vocabulary
>auditory word attack
>auditory discrimina-
  tion
>auditory perception
>auditory memory

Visual skills
>visual reception
>visual association
>visual sequential
  memory
>visual closure
>visual grammatic
  closure
>visual discrimination
>visual perception
>visual memory
>visual eye tracking
>visual eye-hand coor-
  dination
>visual sorting
>figure ground

Motor skills
>fine motor
  gross motor
>sensory motor

Directional skills
  right and left
  up and down
>laterality
>directionality

Modality
>modality
>cross modality

Attention
>visual attention
>auditory attention
>motor attention
>spatial attention

Educational Skills
>tenses
>phonics
>spelling
>sentence structure
  arithmetic
>prefixes
>suffixes
>plurals
>vocabulary
>general information
>thought process
  development
>perceptual consistency
>inner language process
>color discrimination
>conceptual develop-
  ment
>logical reasoning
>numerical discrimina-
  tion
>expression
>differentiating
>decoding
>encoding
>word attack
>retrieval of informa-
  tion
>sequencing
>comprehension
>perseveration
  dictionary skills
>mental agility
>analysis
>synthesis

Social skills
  behavior
  attitude
  winning
  losing
  sharing
  patience
  tolerance
  interactions
  actions
  reactions
  consequences
  appropriate conversa-
    tion
  self control
  self esteem
  impulsiveness
  communication
  compulsiveness
  social perception
  social maturation
  self concept

Memory skills
>short term memory
>sequential memory
>long term memory

121

CONNECT FOUR

Planning your strategy while halting your opponent's brings offensive and defensive skills to the firing line. This game moves quickly and attention is a must! Attention is necessary for eyeing the colors, the spaces, the number of pieces, the order and the sequence of the pieces being played. Awareness, alertness, and all of those good words adding up to your ability to attend are in full swing in Connect Four! This is another marvelous game for learning the value of where you place your attention for your desired results! If you place your attention totally on winning, your opponent will most likely connect his four first. Get ready to think quickly but thoroughly, and your four will connect before your opponent has a chance to notice.

CONNECT FOUR
Skill List

Auditory skills
- >auditory reception
- auditory association
- auditory sequential memory
- auditory closure
- >auditory manual expression
- auditory sound blending
- auditory vocabulary
- auditory word attack
- auditory discrimination
- auditory perception
- auditory memory

Visual skills
- >visual reception
- >visual association
- >visual sequential memory
- >visual closure
- visual grammatic closure
- >visual discrimination
- >visual perception
- >visual memory
- >visual eye tracking
- >visual eye-hand coordination
- visual sorting
- >figure ground

Motor skills
- >fine motor
- gross motor
- >sensory motor

Directional skills
- >right and left
- >up and down
- >laterality
- >directionality

Modality
- >modality
- >cross modality

Attention
- >visual attention
- auditory attention
- >motor attention
- >spatial attention

Educational Skills
- tenses
- phonics
- spelling
- sentence structure
- arithmetic
- prefixes
- suffixes
- plurals
- vocabulary
- >general information
- thought process development
- >perceptual consistency
- inner language process
- >color discrimination
- >conceptual development
- >logical reasoning
- >numerical discrimination
- expression
- >differentiating
- decoding
- encoding
- word attack
- retrieval of information
- >sequencing
- comprehension
- >perseveration
- dictionary skills
- >mental agility
- analysis
- synthesis

Social skills
- behavior
- attitude
- winning
- losing
- sharing
- patience
- tolerance
- interactions
- actions
- reactions
- consequences
- appropriate conversation
- self control
- self esteem
- impulsiveness
- communication
- compulsiveness
- social perception
- social maturation
- self concept

Memory skills
- >short term memory
- >sequential memory
- long term memory

CRIBBAGE

Cribbage is a fabulous game for two people, youngsters, teenagers or adults. It is tough on quick, lateral thinking math skills. It is also tough on math decisions that are unchangeable, once made. Decision making processes need to be practiced where commitment is necessary and this game provides that. Visual, motor, eye-hand coordination, fine motor, counting, pegging and mental agility of math concepts are the skill highlights of Cribbage! Fun, entertainment, pleasure and relaxation are the real noticeable skills! Play Cribbage with or without the children! It is good fun therapy on vacation when activity is slow or you are waiting for remaining members of your party!

Happy, happy pegging!

Chapter XI

CRIBBAGE
Skill List

Auditory skills
>auditory reception
>auditory association
>auditory sequential
  memory
  auditory closure
>auditory manual ex-
  pression
  auditory sound blend-
  ing
  auditory vocabulary
  auditory word attack
  auditory discrimina-
  tion
>auditory perception
>auditory memory

Visual skills
>visual reception
  visual association
>visual sequential
  memory
  visual closure
  visual grammatic
  closure
  visual discrimination
>visual perception
>visual memory
  visual eye tracking
>visual eye-hand coor-
  dination
  visual sorting
  figure ground

Motor skills
>fine motor
  gross motor
>sensory motor

Directional skills
  right and left
  up and down
  laterality
>directionality

Modality
>modality
  cross modality

Attention
>visual attention
>auditory attention
>motor attention
>spatial attention

Educational Skills
  tenses
  phonics
  spelling
  sentence structure
  arithmetic
  prefixes
  suffixes
  plurals
>vocabulary
>general information
>thought process
  development
>perceptual consistency
>inner language process
  color discrimination
>conceptual develop-
  ment
>logical reasoning
>numerical discrimina-
  tion
>expression
>differentiating
  decoding
  encoding
  word attack
>retrieval of informa-
  tion
>sequencing
>comprehension
>perseveration
  dictionary skills
>mental agility
>analysis
>synthesis

Social skills
  behavior
  attitude
  winning
  losing
  sharing
  patience
  tolerance
  interactions
  actions
  reactions
  consequences
  appropriate conversa-
  tion
  self control
  self esteem
  impulsiveness
  communication
  compulsiveness
  social perception
  social maturation
  self concept

Memory skills
>short term memory
>sequential memory
>long term memory

Chapter XI

CROSSWORD/DOMINOES

Get all areas of attention ready to roll with Crossword/Dominoes before it, literally, crosses your eyes. Spatial, visual, motor and auditory attention will certainly be needed as the manipulation of these double lettered tiles become the action in this game. Innerlanguage and innersensory transfer join with long and short term memory as decoding and encoding take over. Sequencing can go in any direction as you synthesize visual, motor, and auditory coordination to retrieve and display sight vocabulary.

The sounding and blending of letters run rampant in the process of mixing, matching, arranging and rearranging for correct spelling. In fact, this game is an in-depth review of all reading and spelling skills. There is enough math to hold your interest while also knowing that an extra fifty points is yours for playing all of your tiles. Keep a dictionary handy to check the exact spelling of words...some opponents get creative...others go insane!

CROSSWORD DOMINOES
Skill List

Auditory skills
auditory reception
>auditory association
>auditory sequential
memory
auditory closure
auditory manual ex-
pression
>auditory sound blend-
ing
auditory vocabulary
>auditory word attack
auditory discrimination
auditory perception
>auditory memory

Visual skills
>visual reception
>visual association
>visual sequential
memory
visual closure
visual grammatic
closure
>visual discrimination
>visual perception
>visual memory
>visual eye tracking
>visual eye-hand coor-
dination
>visual sorting
>figure ground

Motor skills
>fine motor
gross motor
>sensory motor

Directional skills
>right and left
>up and down
>laterality
>directionality

Modality
>modality
>cross modality

Attention
>visual attention
>auditory attention
>motor attention
>spatial attention

Educational Skills
>tenses
>phonics
>spelling
sentence structure
arithmetic
>prefixes
>suffixes
>plurals
>vocabulary
>general information
>thought process
development
>perceptual consistency
>inner language process
color discrimination
conceptual develop-
ment
>logical reasoning
numerical discrimina-
tion
>expression
>differentiating
>decoding
>encoding
>word attack
>retrieval of informa-
tion
>sequencing
>comprehension
>perseveration
>dictionary skills
>mental agility
>analysis
>synthesis

Social skills
behavior
attitude
winning
losing
sharing
patience
tolerance
interactions
actions
reactions
consequences
appropriate conversa-
tion
self control
self esteem
impulsiveness
communication
compulsiveness
social perception
social maturation
self concept

Memory skills
>short term memory
>sequential memory
>long term memory

Chapter XI

DOMINATION

Playing Domination is fun for the beginner, intermediate and expert in this game of strategy and domination. Not only is a player forced to watch the top color on each stack of his pieces and his opponent's stacks, he must also pay attention to the colors in the middle and on the bottom of each stack. Many visual skills are involved such as visual discrimination, visual sorting of all the pieces, visual memory of where your pieces are located, and visual association of all the different pieces on the board. A great deal of eye tracking is combined with color discrimination as you eye all of the moving pieces. Eye-hand coordination, fine motor skills, directionality and laterality are also active skills as you move each piece. Along with this and throughout the game, the mental processes of visual attention, motor attention and spatial attention are all present. Like most games short-term memory is involved in remembering all the different rules to be followed. Although Domination is a game of strategy, it can be played on a lighter note and enjoyed. Remember it is not how many of your pieces that are on the board that counts, the final clincher is that you are on the top. It is possible to be knocked out of the game and then return later in the game when your color reappears. Remember, do not get caught on the bottom!

DOMINATION
Skill List

Auditory skills
>auditory reception
auditory association
auditory sequential
  memory
auditory closure
>auditory manual ex-
  pression
auditory sound blend-
  ing
auditory vocabulary
auditory word attack
auditory discrimination
auditory perception
auditory memory

Visual skills
>visual reception
visual association
visual sequential
  memory
visual closure
visual grammatic
  closure
>visual discrimination
visual perception
>visual memory
>visual eye tracking
>visual eye-hand coor-
  dination
visual sorting
figure ground

Motor skills
>fine motor
gross motor
sensory motor

Directional skills
>right and left
>up and down
>laterality
>directionality

Modality
>modality
cross modality

Attention
>visual attention
auditory attention
>motor attention
>spatial attention

Educational Skills
tenses
phonics
spelling
sentence structure
>arithmetic
prefixes
suffixes
plurals
vocabulary
>general information
>thought process
  development
>perceptual consistency
>inner language process
>color discrimination
>conceptual develop-
  ment
>logical reasoning
>numerical discrimina-
  tion
expression
differentiating
decoding
encoding
word attack
retrieval of informa-
  tion
sequencing
comprehension
perseveration
dictionary skills
>mental agility
>analysis
>synthesis

Social skills
behavior
attitude
winning
losing
sharing
patience
tolerance
interactions
actions
reactions
consequences
appropriate conversa-
  tion
self control
self esteem
impulsiveness
communication
compulsiveness
social perception
social maturation
self concept

Memory skills
>short term memory
sequential memory
>long term memory

DOMINOES

Dominoes have been around so long that they now come without instructions! These little dotted pieces come in double sixes or in double nines. Buy both and begin play with the sixes. As soon as the skills are mastered for these, move on to the nines. They can even be mixed for more confusing fun at a later date. Children can avoid being tutored in addition and subtraction facts if enough games like Dominoes are played in the home. The combinations become automatic more quickly with the added stimulus of play. Counting up your points is marvelous practice in addition, and subtracting your playing piece is another good mental math process.

Dominoes offer excellent practice for many of the visual skills. Fine motor, mental agility, differentiation and attention are all requirements for a good game.

DOMINOES
Skill List

Auditory skills
>auditory reception
 auditory association
>auditory sequential
 memory
 auditory closure
>auditory manual ex-
 pression
 auditory sound blend-
 ing
 auditory vocabulary
 auditory word attack
 auditory discrimina-
 tion
>auditory perception
>auditory memory

Visual skills
>visual reception
>visual association
>visual sequential
 memory
 visual closure
 visual grammatic
 closure
>visual discrimination
>visual perception
>visual memory
>visual eye tracking
>visual eye-hand coor-
 dination
>visual sorting
 figure ground

Motor skills
>fine motor
 gross motor
>sensory motor

Directional skills
>right and left
>up and down
>laterality
>directionality

Modality
>modality
>cross modality

Attention
>visual attention
>auditory attention
>motor attention
>spatial attention

Educational Skills
 tenses
 phonics
 spelling
 sentence structure
>arithmetic
 prefixes
 suffixes
 plurals
 vocabulary
>general information
>thought process
 development
>perceptual consistency
 inner language process
>color discrimination
>conceptual develop-
 ment
>logical reasoning
>numerical discrimina-
 tion
>expression
>differentiating
 decoding
 encoding
 word attack
>retrieval of informa-
 tion
>sequencing
>comprehension
>perseveration
 dictionary skills
 mental agility
>analysis

>synthesis

Social skills
 behavior
 attitude
 winning
 losing
 sharing
 patience
 tolerance
 interactions
 actions
 reactions
 consequences
 appropriate conversa-
 tion
 self control
 self esteem
 impulsiveness
 communication
 compulsiveness
 social perception
 social maturation
 self concept

Memory skills
>short term memory
>sequential memory
>long term memory

DUNGEON DICE

Oh to be free...this desire becomes a monstrosity in your mind as you hope for Dungeon Dice to free you from the cold, dark dungeon. Who would ever realize that learning useful skills is taking place when attention is so strongly placed on freedom? The daggers, keys, shovels, ladders and lanterns are possibilities every role...possibilities that pave the way for your great escape. It takes strategy to avoid the gruesome guards and prisoners who are always there to halt your progress. Yes, in and among this excitement you find skills that enhance learning. We wish victory for you as you dig your way out of the dark and dismal dungeon -- a smarter person with new skills.

Chapter XI

DUNGEON DICE
Skill List

Auditory skills
auditory reception
auditory association
auditory sequential
  memory
auditory closure
>auditory manual ex-
  pression
auditory sound blend-
  ing
auditory vocabulary
auditory word attack
auditory discrimination
auditory perception
>auditory memory

Visual skills
>visual reception
>visual association
visual sequential
  memory
visual closure
visual grammatic
  closure
>visual discrimination
>visual perception
>visual memory
>visual eye tracking
>visual eye-hand coor-
  dination
>visual sorting
>figure ground

Motor skills
>fine motor
gross motor
sensory motor

Directional skills
right and left
up and down
>laterality
>directionality

Modality
>modality
cross modality

Attention
>visual attention
auditory attention
>motor attention
>spatial attention

Educational Skills
>tenses
>phonics
>spelling
sentence structure
arithmetic
>prefixes
>suffixes
>plurals
vocabulary
>general information
>thought process
  development
>perceptual consistency
>inner language process
color discrimination
conceptual develop-
  ment
>logical reasoning
numerical discrimina-
  tion
expression
>differentiating
>decoding
>encoding
>word attack
>retrieval of informa-
  tion
>sequencing
>comprehension
>perseveration
>dictionary skills
>mental agility
>analysis
>synthesis

Social skills
behavior
attitude
winning
losing
sharing
patience
tolerance
interactions
actions
reactions
consequences
appropriate conversa-
  tion
self control
self esteem
impulsiveness
communication
compulsiveness
social perception
social maturation
self concept

Memory skills
>short term memory
>sequential memory
long term memory

133

Chapter XI

ESP MIND FORCE

Oh my! Have you ever heard of mind force in a game? It is different because it allows your mind to take over and cause strange things to happen. The board and the special finger marker work in mysterious ways. One or two people can play but we suggest two instead of one because who will believe your story if no one is there to see those strange---things---happening! Skills? What skills? This game is using your mind...brain...and energy. The instructions offer interesting information for your reading pleasure on: Bio-Rhythms, Clairvoyance, Precognition and Prediction Pendulum! Does this description sufficiently arouse your interest? It does ours! STRANGE HAPPENINGS ARE OCCURRING! GUESS THE SKILLS AS YOU PLAY!

Chapter XI

ESP MIND FORCE
Skill List

Auditory skills
auditory reception
auditory association
auditory sequential
  memory
auditory closure
auditory manual ex-
  pression
auditory sound blend-
  ing
auditory vocabulary
auditory word attack
auditory discrimina-
  tion
auditory perception
auditory memory

Visual skills
visual reception
visual association
visual sequential
  memory
visual closure
visual grammatic
  closure
visual discrimination
visual perception
visual memory
visual eye tracking
visual eye-hand coor-
  dination
visual sorting
figure ground

Motor skills
fine motor
gross motor
sensory motor

Directional skills
right and left
up and down
laterality
directionality

Modality
modality
cross modality

Attention
visual attention
auditory attention
motor attention
spatial attention

Educational Skills
tenses
phonics
spelling
sentence structure
arithmetic
prefixes
suffixes
plurals
vovcabulary
general information
thought process
  development
perceptual consistency
inner language process
color discrimination
conceptual develop-
  ment
logical reasoning
numerical discrimina-
  tion
expression
differentiating
decoding
encoding
word attack
retrieval of informa-
  tion
sequencing
comprehension
perseveration
dictionary skills
mental agility
analysis

synthesis

Social skills
behavior
attitude
winning
losing
sharing
patience
tolerance
interactions
actions
reactions
consequences
appropriate conversa-
  tion
self control
self esteem
impulsiveness
communication
compulsiveness
social perception
social maturation
self concept

Memory skills
short term memory
sequential memory
long term memory

Chapter XI

FAMILY FEUD

Even though Richard Dawson does not come running out to kiss you as you open the box, Family Feud is a good auditory skill builder. Auditory memory, association and expression are well enforced along with the many visual skills involved in reading.

This game is a stretching exercise for both long and short term memory. Family Feud provides phenomenal practice in quick thinking of exact vocabulary and/or synonymous phrases. It requires your attention and awareness at all times. As you mentally store the answers your opponents are giving, you must also be thinking some of your own...just in case! This is a tremendous exercise for the brain in lateral thinking.

Good answer! Good answer!

Chapter XI

FAMILY FEUD
Skill List

Auditory skills
>auditory reception
>auditory association
>auditory sequential
  memory
>auditory closure
>auditory manual expression
>auditory sound blending
>auditory vocabulary
>auditory word attack
>auditory discrimination
>auditory perception
>auditory memory

Visual skills
>visual reception
>visual association
>visual sequential
  memory
>visual closure
>visual grammatic
  closure
>visual discrimination
>visual perception
>visual memory
>visual eye tracking
>visual eye-hand coordination
>visual sorting
>figure ground

Motor skills
>fine motor
>gross motor
>sensory motor

Directional skills
>right and left
>up and down
>laterality
>directionality

Modality
>modality
>cross modality

Attention
>visual attention
>auditory attention
>motor attention
>spatial attention

Educational Skills
>tenses
>phonics
>spelling
>sentence structure
  arithmetic
>prefixes
>suffixes
>plurals
>vocabulary
>general information
>thought process
  development
>perceptual consistency
>inner language process
  color discrimination
>conceptual development
>logical reasoning
  numerical discrimination
>expression
>differentiating
>decoding
>encoding
>word attack
>retrieval of information
>sequencing
>comprehension
>perseveration
>dictionary skills
>mental agility
>analysis
>synthesis

Social skills
behavior
attitude
winning
losing
sharing
patience
tolerance
interactions
actions
reactions
consequences
appropriate conversation
self control
self esteem
impulsiveness
communication
compulsiveness
social perception
social maturation
self concept

Memory skills
>short term memory
>sequential memory
>long term memory

GAME OF THE STATES

This game provides a simple way of gaining perspective on the name and location of each state and capital. Additional information concerning industry and raw materials is available. Much learning occurs quickly in this geographical game.

Spatial, motor, visual and auditory attention are required as you travel from state to state. Many visual and auditory skills are being rehearsed as you take your trip around the United States of America. Be careful of disasters like having a breakdown, giving out of gas, or having a flat tire! In such cases, you may lose your turn or lose the product you are delivering. Happy traveling! See you in Hawaii!

Chapter XI

GAME OF THE STATES
Skill List

Auditory skills
>auditory reception
>auditory association
auditory sequential
memory
>auditory closure
>auditory manual ex-
pression
>auditory sound blend-
ing
>auditory vocabulary
>auditory word attack
>auditory discrimination
>auditory perception
>auditory memory

Visual skills
>visual reception
>visual association
>visual sequential
memory
>visual closure
>visual grammatic
closure
>visual discrimination
>visual perception
>visual memory
>visual eye tracking
>visual eye-hand coor-
dination
>visual sorting
>figure ground

Motor skills
>fine motor
gross motor
sensory motor

Directional skills
>right and left
>up and down
>laterality
>directionality

Modality
>modality
>cross modality

Attention
>visual attention
>auditory attention
>motor attention
>spatial attention

Educational Skills
tenses
phonics
spelling
>sentence structure
arithmetic
prefixes
suffixes
plurals
vocabulary
>general information
>thought process
development
>perceptual consistency
>inner language process
color discrimination
>conceptual develop-
ment
>logical reasoning
numerical discrimina-
tion
>expression
>differentiating
>decoding
>encoding
>word attack
>retrieval of informa-
tion
sequencing
>comprehension
>perseveration
dictionary skills
>mental agility
>analysis
>synthesis

Social skills
behavior
attitude
winning
losing
sharing
patience
tolerance
interactions
actions
reactions
consequences
appropriate conversa-
tion
self control
self esteem
impulsiveness
communication
compulsiveness
social perception
social maturation
self concept

Memory skills
>short term memory
>sequential memory
>long term memory

139

GO TO THE HEAD OF THE CLASS

Answer questions! Get smart, while you are still young. All subjects and all kinds of questions are available for your learning. This, of course, offers all reading skills, auditory skills and visual skills as you practice playing the game. Cross modality and visual integration are actively involved. Long-term and short-term memory are a strong part of this game. Try these two sample questions on for size. If you are sharp enough you will receive an A. "Who would be more interested in a tutu, a golfer or a ballerina?" "What are you using if you are using your noodle?" It is time to use it now...right now!

Chapter XI

GO TO THE HEAD OF THE CLASS
Skill List

Auditory skills
>auditory reception
>auditory association
>auditory sequential
  memory
>auditory closure
>auditory manual ex-
  pression
>auditory sound blend-
  ing
>auditory vocabulary
>auditory word attack
>auditory discrimina-
  tion
>auditory perception
>auditory memory

Visual skills
>visual reception
>visual association
>visual sequential
  memory
>visual closure
>visual grammatic
  closure
>visual discrimination
>visual perception
>visual memory
>visual eye tracking
>visual eye-hand coor-
  dination
>visual sorting
>figure ground

Motor skills
>fine motor
  gross motor
>sensory motor

Directional skills
  right and left
  up and down
>laterality
>directionality

Modality
>modality
>cross modality

Attention
>visual attention
>auditory attention
>motor attention
>spatial attention

Educational Skills
>tenses
>phonics
>spelling
>sentence structure
  arithmetic
>prefixes
>suffixes
>plurals
>vocabulary
>general information
>thought process
  development
  perceptual consistency
>inner language process
  color discrimination
>conceptual develop-
  ment
>logical reasoning
  numerical discrimina-
  tion
>expression
>differentiating
>decoding
>encoding
>word attack
>retrieval of informa-
  tion
>sequencing
>comprehension
>perseveration
>dictionary skills
>mental agility
>analysis
>synthesis

Social skills
  behavior
  attitude
  winning
  losing
  sharing
  patience
  tolerance
  interactions
  actions
  reactions
  consequences
  appropriate conversa-
  tion
  self control
  self esteem
  impulsiveness
  communication
  compulsiveness
  social perception
  social maturation
  self concept

Memory skills
>short term memory
>sequential memory
>long term memory

HANNIBAL

This game may still be around your house, and if so it is a good game for visual attention, counting, simple decision making and visual memory. Patience is important, too, if rolling the correct number is difficult near the end of the game. Color coordination is involved and strategy evolves from deciding which ones to stack and unstack for single or group moving. Sounds different, does it not?

Chapter XI

HANNIBAL
Skill List

Auditory skills
>auditory reception
auditory association
auditory sequential
  memory
auditory closure
>auditory manual expression
auditory sound blending
auditory vocabulary
auditory word attack
auditory discrimination
auditory perception
>auditory memory

Visual skills
>visual reception
visual association
visual sequential
  memory
visual closure
visual grammatic
  closure
>visual discrimination
>visual perception
>visual memory
>visual eye tracking
>visual eye-hand coordination
>visual sorting
figure ground

Motor skills
>fine motor
gross motor
sensory motor

Directional skills
right and left
up and down
>laterality
>directionality

Modality
>modality
cross modality

Attention
>visual attention
auditory attention
>motor attention
>spatial attention

Educational Skills
tenses
phonics
spelling
sentence structure
arithmetic
prefixes
suffixes
plurals
vocabulary
general information
thought process
  development
perceptual consistency
inner language process
color discrimination
conceptual development
logical reasoning
numerical discrimination
expression
>differentiating
decoding
encoding
word attack
retrieval of information
>sequencing
>comprehension
perseveration
dictionary skills
mental agility
analysis
synthesis

Social skills
behavior
attitude
winning
losing
sharing
patience
tolerance
interactions
actions
reactions
consequences
appropriate conversation
self control
self esteem
impulsiveness
communication
compulsiveness
social perception
social maturation
self concept

Memory skills
>short term memory
sequential memory
>long term memory

143

HEADACHE

Visual tracking is a large part of the Pop-O-Matic game called Headache, as each player follows his pieces and those of others around the board. Fine motor and eye-hand coordination are used not only in moving the pieces, but also in pushing the dice popper... this game actually builds finger muscles! Many visual skills are present as you watch the board. Visual motor, visual perception, visual association, and visual memory are in constant use. Strategy is also involved in trying to capture the pieces of the other players. Directionality comes into action in determining which way to move, along with counting the movements of each piece. Visual, motor, and spatial attention are used in watching the board. The pieces and the board are of many colors which enhances the use of color coordination and color discrimination. This is an easy game to learn, yet challenging and fun for each and every player. It is time to get your aspirin ready!

HEADACHE
Skill List

Auditory skills
>auditory reception
 auditory association
 auditory sequential
  memory
 auditory closure
>auditory manual ex-
  pression
 auditory sound blend-
  ing
>auditory vocabulary
 auditory word attack
 auditory discrimina-
  tion
>auditory perception
>auditory memory

Visual skills
>visual reception
>visual association
>visual sequential
  memory
 visual closure
 visual grammatic
  closure
>visual discrimination
>visual perception
>visual memory
>visual eye tracking
>visual eye-hand coor-
  dination
 visual sorting
 figure ground

Motor skills
>fine motor
 gross motor
 sensory motor

Directional skills
 right and left
 up and down
 laterality
>directionality

Modality
>modality
 cross modality

Attention
>visual attention
>auditory attention
>motor attention
>spatial attention

Educational Skills
 tenses
 phonics
 spelling
 sentence structure
>arithmetic
 prefixes
 suffixes
 plurals
 vocabulary
>general information
>thought process
  development
>perceptual consistency
 inner language process
>color discrimination
 conceptual develop-
  ment
>logical reasoning
 numerical discrimina-
  tion
>expression
 differentiating
 decoding
 encoding
 word attack
>retrieval of informa-
  tion
 sequencing
 comprehension
 perseveration
 dictionary skills
>mental agility
>analysis
 synthesis

Social skills
 behavior
 attitude
 winning
 losing
 sharing
 patience
 tolerance
 interactions
 actions
 reactions
 consequences
 appropriate conversa-
  tion
 self control
 self esteem
 impulsiveness
 communication
 compulsiveness
 social perception
 social maturation
 self concept

Memory skills
>short term memory
>sequential memory
>long term memory

HEAD TO TOE

This game is like no other on the market today! It blends a set of spatial skills rarely found in games. Directionality, fine motor and perception are working in conjunction with visual attention and other visual skills. These skills are invaluable in placing the correct body parts on the right person. Head To Toe not only teaches body positions, it also intertwines strategies as you arrange arms, hands, heads and other body parts to build each person. It is a great game for all ages. Just imagine! After playing this game your I.Q. may go higher...your "draw a man" skills will improve!

Chapter XI

HEAD TO TOE
Skill List

Auditory skills
>auditory reception
>auditory association
auditory sequential memory
auditory closure
>auditory manual expression
auditory sound blending
>auditory vocabulary
auditory word attack
>auditory discrimination
>auditory perception
>auditory memory

Visual skills
>visual reception
>visual association
>visual sequential memory
visual closure
visual grammatic closure
>visual discrimination
>visual perception
>visual memory
>visual eye tracking
>visual eye-hand coordination
>visual sorting
>figure ground

Motor skills
>fine motor
gross motor
sensory motor

Directional skills
>right and left
>up and down
>front and behind
>laterality
>directionality

Modality
>modality
>cross modality

Attention
>visual attention
>auditory attention
>motor attention
>spatial attention

Educational Skills
tenses
phonics
spelling
sentence structure
arithmetic
prefixes
suffixes
plurals
vocabulary
>general information
>thought process development
>perceptual consistency
>inner language process
>color discrimination
>conceptual development
>logical reasoning
numerical discrimination
>expression
>differentiating
decoding
encoding
word attack
>retrieval of information
>sequencing
>comprehension
>perseveration
dictionary skills
>mental agility
>analysis
>synthesis

Social skills
behavior
attitude
winning
losing
sharing
patience
tolerance
interactions
actions
reactions
consequences
appropriate conversation
self control
self esteem
impulsiveness
communication
compulsiveness
social perception
social maturation
self concept

Memory skills
>short term memory
>sequential memory
>long term memory

INNER CIRCLE

This little game tickles the brain! Luck has a very small role in Inner Circle because strategy begins with your very first move. Deductive reasoning, logical processing and heavy strategy are of utmost importance! Even so, these deep processes are of little value without the extension of short term memory. This memory allows you to recall the numbers under your men and to know how to plan your future moves. Attention and memory get a real workout in the visual, motor and spatial areas.

Put your skills and brain to spinning,

as you see your chances thinning.

Visualize yourself the winner,

and in last circle you will enter!

Chapter XI

INNER CIRCLE
Skill List

Auditory skills
>auditory reception
>auditory association
>auditory sequential
 memory
 auditory closure
>auditory manual ex-
 pression
 auditory sound blend-
 ing
 auditory vocabulary
 auditory word attack
 auditory discrimina-
 tion
>auditory perception
>auditory memory

Visual skills
>visual reception
>visual association
>visual sequential
 memory
>visual closure
 visual grammatic
 closure
>visual discrimination
>visual perception
>visual memory
>visual eye tracking
>visual eye-hand coor-
 dination
>visual sorting
>figure ground

Motor skills
>fine motor
 gross motor
 sensory motor

Directional skills
 right and left
 up and down
>laterality
>directionality

Modality
>modality
>cross modality

Attention
>visual attention
 auditory attention
>motor attention
>spatial attention

Educational Skills
 tenses
 phonics
 spelling
 sentence structure
 arithmetic
 prefixes
 suffixes
 plurals
 vocabulary
>general information
>thought process
 development
>perceptual consistency
 inner language process
>color discrimination
>conceptual develop-
 ment
>logical reasoning
 numerical discrimina-
 tion
 expression
>differentiating
 decoding
 encoding
 word attack
 retrieval of informa-
 tion
>sequencing
>comprehension
>perseveration
 dictionary skills
>mental agility
 analysis
>synthesis

Social skills
 behavior
 attitude
 winning
 losing
 sharing
 patience
 tolerance
 interactions
 actions
 reactions
 consequences
 appropriate conversa-
 tion
 self control
 self esteem
 impulsiveness
 communication
 compulsiveness
 social perception
 social maturation
 self concept

Memory skills
>short term memory
>sequential memory
>long term memory

Chapter XI

IPSWITCH

Oopswitch is another possibility for a title! When your opponents retain the best letters and pass the leftovers on to you, word building gets interesting, perplexing, confusing and terribly complex...if not impossible!! This game certainly offers new and amusing ways to review your word attack skills. Manipulating sounds, blends, digraphs and phonemes for building new words are important skills in Ipswitch. Vocabulary and spelling are on the rise in this game. Good math skills are interwoven also in the complex scoring process. Patience and attention are stretched thoroughly since each play is allowed a ten minute time limit! It is marvelous to enjoy practicing skills for ten minutes! This game is appropriate for a wide range of age levels!

Get those visual skills and "internal auditories" up and going! Action avoids penalties and builds bonus points!

Chapter XI

IPSWITCH
Skill List

Auditory skills
>auditory reception
>auditory association
>auditory sequential
   memory
>auditory closure
>auditory manual ex-
   pression
>auditory sound blend-
   ing
>auditory vocabulary
>auditory word attack
>auditory discrimination
>auditory perception
>auditory memory

Visual skills
>visual reception
>visual association
>visual sequential
   memory
>visual closure
>visual grammatic
   closure
>visual discrimination
>visual perception
>visual memory
>visual eye tracking
>visual eye-hand coor-
   dination
>visual sorting
>figure ground

Motor skills
>fine motor
   gross motor
>sensory motor

Directional skills
   right and left
   up and down
>laterality
>directionality

Modality
>modality
>cross modality

Attention
>visual attention
>auditory attention
>motor attention
>spatial attention

Educational Skills
>tenses
>phonics
>spelling
   sentence structure
   arithmetic
>prefixes
>suffixes
>plurals
>vocabulary
>general information
>thought process
   development
>perceptual consistency
>inner language process
   color discrimination
   conceptual develop-
   ment
>logical reasoning
   numerical discrimina-
   tion
>expression
>differentiating
>decoding
>encoding
>word attack
>retrieval of informa-
   tion
>sequencing
>comprehension
>perseveration
>dictionary skills
>mental agility
>analysis
>synthesis

Social skills
   behavior
   attitude
   winning
   losing
   sharing
   patience
   tolerance
   interactions
   actions
   reactions
   consequences
   appropriate conversa-
   tion
   self control
   self esteem
   impulsiveness
   communication
   compulsiveness
   social perception
   social maturation
   self concept

Memory skills
>short term memory
>sequential memory
>long term memory

151

JACKPOT YAHTZEE

Visual perception, sorting and visual discrimination combine with spatial, motor and visual attention to keep you dreaming of the jackpot! This game involves choices and decision making that become a serious matter. The idea of a "spare" causes additional factors to enter into your mental processing of number manipulation.

Scoring is another set of skills, as is learning the meaning of the combinations on your dice. Jackpot Yahtzee does keep you thinking! Part of your strategy in this game becomes deciding what to do with your luck. Good luck!

Chapter XI

JACKPOT YAHTZEE
Skill List

Auditory skills
>auditory reception
auditory association
>auditory sequential
memory
auditory closure
>auditory manual expression
auditory sound blending
auditory vocabulary
auditory word attack
auditory discrimination
>auditory perception
>auditory memory

Visual skills
>visual reception
>visual association
visual sequential
memory
visual closure
visual grammatic
closure
>visual discrimination
>visual perception
visual memory
visual eye tracking
>visual eye-hand coordination
>visual sorting
figure ground

Motor skills
>fine motor
gross motor
sensory motor

Directional skills
>right and left
>up and down
>laterality
>directionality

Modality
>modality
cross modality

Attention
>visual attention
auditory attention
>motor attention
>spatial attention

Educational Skills
tenses
phonics
spelling
sentence structure
>arithmetic
prefixes
suffixes
plurals
vocabulary
general information
thought process
development
>perceptual consistency
inner language process
>color discrimination
conceptual development
>logical reasoning
>numerical discrimination
expression
>differentiating
decoding
encoding
word attack
>retrieval of information
>sequencing
comprehension
perseveration
dictionary skills
mental agility
>analysis
synthesis

Social skills
behavior
attitude
winning
losing
sharing
patience
tolerance
interactions
actions
reactions
consequences
appropriate conversation
self control
self esteem
impulsiveness
communication
compulsiveness
social perception
social maturation
self concept

Memory skills
>short term memory
>sequential memory
>long term memory

JENGA

Jenga is a special game for the development of fine motor skills especially in the sensitivity of touch. The object of this game is to remove blocks from somewhere in the stack below the top level and to replace each block on the very top while keeping the stack from falling. In this process a player must think in terms of action/reaction in order to determine whether or not the block he wants to remove will result in the stack tumbling down. It is a fun filled game that includes the skills of visual, spatial and motor attention as you watch the stack become more and more unsteady. Visual and spatial perception are used in deciding which block to remove. Jenga creates judgment, decision making processes, and a good sense of eye-hand coordination. Anxiety and stress are present in this game but they combine with the feeling that it is okay to lose. This is a game that makes you laugh as the stack teeters higher and higher before the big crash.

Chapter XI

JENGA
Skill List

Auditory skills
>auditory reception
auditory association
auditory sequential
memory
auditory closure
>auditory manual ex-
pression
auditory sound blend-
ing
auditory vocabulary
auditory word attack
auditory discrimina-
tion
auditory perception
>auditory memory

Visual skills
>visual reception
visual association
visual sequential
memory
visual closure
visual grammatic
closure
visual discrimination
>visual perception
>visual memory
>visual eye tracking
>visual eye-hand coor-
dination
visual sorting
figure ground

Motor skills
>fine motor
gross motor
>sensory motor

Directional skills
>right and left
>up and down
>laterality
>directionality

Modality
>modality
>cross modality

Attention
>visual attention
auditory attention
>motor attention
>spatial attention

Educational Skills
tenses
phonics
spelling
sentence structure
arithmetic
prefixes
suffixes
plurals
vocabulary
>general information
>thought process
development
>perceptual consistency
inner language process
color discrimination
>conceptual develop-
ment
>logical reasoning
numerical discrimina-
tion
expression
differentiating
decoding
encoding
word attack
retrieval of informa-
tion
>sequencing
comprehension
>perseveration
dictionary skills
>mental agility
analysis
synthesis

Social skills
behavior
attitude
winning
losing
sharing
patience
tolerance
interactions
actions
reactions
consequences
appropriate conversa-
tion
self control
self esteem
impulsiveness
communication
compulsiveness
social perception
social maturation
self concept

Memory skills
>short term memory
>sequential memory
>long term memory

155

LAST WORD

Last word allows your imagination to spiral in any direction, north, south, east, west or skyward. From directionality you move into your memory bank to retrieve every word attack skill that you have deposited there.

Hundreds of skills come forth and blend to assist you in building your words higher and higher. Visual, internal auditory, spatial and motor skills all combine to allow you processing that culminates in perfect word construction. Get ready to spell toward the sky!

Chapter XI

LAST WORD
Skill List

Auditory skills
>auditory reception
>auditory association
>auditory sequential memory
>auditory closure
>auditory manual expression
>auditory sound blending
>auditory vocabulary
>auditory word attack
>auditory discrimination
>auditory perception
>auditory memory

Visual skills
>visual reception
>visual association
>visual sequential memory
>visual closure
>visual grammatic closure
>visual discrimination
>visual perception
>visual memory
>visual eye tracking
>visual eye-hand coordination
>visual sorting
>figure ground

Motor skills
>fine motor
gross motor
>sensory motor

Directional skills
>right and left
>up and down
>laterality
>directionality

Modality
>modality
>cross modality

Attention
>visual attention
>auditory attention
>motor attention
>spatial attention

Educational Skills
>tenses
>phonics
>spelling
sentence structure
arithmetic
>prefixes
>suffixes
>plurals
>vocabulary
>general information
>thought process development
>perceptual consistency
>inner language process
color discrimination
>conceptual development
logical reasoning
numerical discrimination
expression
>differentiating
>decoding
>encoding
>word attack
>retrieval of information
>sequencing
>comprehension
>perseveration
>dictionary skills
>mental agility
>analysis
>synthesis

Social skills
behavior
attitude
winning
losing
sharing
patience
tolerance
interactions
actions
reactions
consequences
appropriate conversation
self control
self esteem
impulsiveness
communication
compulsiveness
social perception
social maturation
self concept

Memory skills
>short term memory
>sequential memory
>long term memory

LIFE

This game offers us a funny reminder of some common realities of everyday life. Although marriage and having children is forced upon you, you often find yourself motoring along with your family facing one dilemma after another.

Life offers extensive practice in coordination of color, hand and eye. Visual skills including perception, memory and discrimination are present. All word attack skills and auditory ones are called for in the game of Life as they are in real life. All attentions are useful in this game including visual, auditory, spatial and motor. Adding and subtracting large numbers provides good mathematical concepts. Directionality runs in circles and so do you before you finally pass your day of reckoning and become a millionaire. What a Life!

LIFE
Skill List

Auditory skills
>auditory reception
auditory association
auditory sequential
  memory
auditory closure
>auditory manual ex-
  pression
auditory sound blend-
  ing
>auditory vocabulary
auditory word attack
auditory discrimina-
  tion
auditory perception
>auditory memory

Visual skills
>visual reception
visual association
>visual sequential
  memory
visual closure
visual grammatic
  closure
>visual discrimination
>visual perception
>visual memory
>visual eye tracking
>visual eye-hand coor-
  dination
>visual sorting
figure ground

Motor skills
>fine motor
gross motor
>sensory motor

Directional skills
>right and left
up and down
laterality
>directionality

Modality
>modality
>cross modality

Attention
>visual attention
>auditory attention
>motor attention
>spatial attention

Educational Skills
tenses
phonics
spelling
>sentence structure
>arithmetic
>prefixes
>suffixes
>plurals
>vocabulary
>general information
>thought process
  development
>perceptual consistency
>inner language process
>color discrimination
>conceptual develop-
  ment
>logical reasoning
>numerical discrimina-
  tion
>expression
>differentiating
>decoding
>encoding
>word attack
>retrieval of informa-
  tion
>sequencing
>comprehension
>perseveration
dictionary skills
>mental agility
>analysis
>synthesis

Social skills
behavior
attitude
winning
losing
sharing
patience
tolerance
interactions
actions
reactions
consequences
appropriate conversa-
  tion
self control
self esteem
impulsiveness
communication
compulsiveness
social perception
social maturation
self concept

Memory skills
>short term memory
sequential memory
>long term memory

Chapter XI

MARBLES

An old fashioned game of Marbles is something most people rarely think of anymore. We have! Marbles is a great game. It is fun, challenging and it gets one down on the ground playing in the dirt. Kids will love it. An unusual hand movement is used as you shoot the marble, developing muscles that most games overlook. This process develops a fine motor skill unlike any other. Gross motor skills are also used as you crawl around on the ground or floor, under tables or "whatever" is in your way while you are trying to chase down the marbles or setting one up for a shot. Spatial attention, motor attention and visual perception are used along with eye-hand coordination in watching the marbles and shooting them. The object is to collect as many marbles as possible without losing your own. The conversations you have when playing can become quite funny as the marbles sail around, so do not be afraid of letting loose.

MARBLES
Skill List

Auditory skills
auditory reception
auditory association
auditory sequential
  memory
auditory closure
>auditory manual expression
auditory sound blending
auditory vocabulary
auditory word attack
auditory discrimination
>auditory perception
>auditory memory

Visual skills
>visual reception
visual association
visual sequential
  memory
visual closure
visual grammatic
  closure
>visual discrimination
>visual perception
>visual memory
>visual eye tracking
>visual eye-hand coordination
visual sorting
figure ground

Motor skills
>fine motor
>gross motor
sensory motor

Directional skills
>right and left
up and down
>laterality
>directionality

Modality
>modality
>cross modality

Attention
>visual attention
auditory attention
>motor attention
>spatial attention

Educational Skills
tenses
phonics
spelling
sentence structure
arithmetic
prefixes
suffixes
plurals
vocabulary
general information
thought process
  development
>perceptual consistency
inner language process
color discrimination
>conceptual development
>logical reasoning
numerical discrimination
expression
>differentiating
decoding
encoding
word attack
>retrieval of information
sequencing
comprehension
>perseveration
dictionary skills
>mental agility
analysis
>synthesis

Social skills
behavior
attitude
winning
losing
sharing
patience
tolerance
interactions
actions
reactions
consequences
appropriate conversation
self control
self esteem
impulsiveness
communication
compulsiveness
social perception
social maturation
self concept

Memory skills
>short term memory
sequential memory
>long term memory

Chapter XI

MASTER MIND AND SUPER MASTER MIND

Master Mind and Super Master Mind are both fun
and challenging for two people. These games are strong
builders of color coordination skills and strategy development. A great deal of short term memory and visual perception are used in the logical deductive reasoning tasks of
these two games. They also stretch the player's mind as one
visually sorts all of the information to be analyzed. Eye-hand
coordination and fine motor skills are involved in pegging
the pieces. These games are strongest in building a foundation or base for analyzing information and drawing con-
clusions. The amount of practice in deductive reasoning and
decision making is absolutely marvelous in each of these
games. Master Mind and Super Master Mind offer the perfect setting for intense practice in conceptualizing. Get ready
for stretching the brain and for filling it with new strategies.

Chapter XI

MASTER MIND AND SUPER MASTER MIND
Skill List

Auditory skills
>auditory reception
>auditory association
>auditory sequential
  memory
  auditory closure
>auditory manual ex-
  pression
  auditory sound blend-.
  ing
  auditory vocabulary
  auditory word attack
>auditory discrimina-
  tion
>auditory perception
>auditory memory

Visual skills
>visual reception
>visual association
>visual sequential
  memory
>visual closure
>visual grammatic
  closure
>visual discrimination
>visual perception
>visual memory
>visual eye tracking
>visual eye-hand coor-
  dination
>visual sorting
>figure ground

Motor skills
>fine motor
  gross motor
>sensory motor

Directional skills
  right and left
  up and down
>laterality
>directionality

Modality
>modality
>cross modality

Attention
>visual attention
>auditory attention
>motor attention
>spatial attention

Educational Skills
  tenses
  phonics
  spelling
>sentence structure
  arithmetic
  prefixes
  suffixes
  plurals
  vocabulary
>general information
>thought process
  development
>perceptual consistency
>inner language process
>color discrimination
>conceptual develop-
  ment
>logical reasoning
  numerical discrimina-
  tion
>expression
>differentiating
>decoding
  encoding
  word attack
>retrieval of informa-
  tion
>sequencing
>comprehension
>perseveration
  dictionary skills
>mental agility
>analysis
>synthesis

Social skills
  behavior
  attitude
  winning
  losing
  sharing
  patience
  tolerance
  interactions
  actions
  reactions
  consequences
  appropriate conversa-
  tion
  self control
  self esteem
  impulsiveness
  communication
  compulsiveness
  social perception
  social maturation
  self concept

Memory skills
>short term memory
>sequential memory
>long term memory

163

MEMO

Memo is a wonderful game for developing short-term memory. In this game a number of cards are turned face down and the object is to choose pairs of cards that match. It forces a person to stretch his visual memory by remembering which cards he has seen. Directionality and spatial attention enable the player to recall the locations of the cards. Whether the direction is up, down, or side by side needs to be remembered. His visual attention is also used in building a strategy to remember which picture is on the card and where the matching card is located. In looking at the cards a number of skills are active, including visual discrimination, visual association, visual sorting and visual perception. Skills of fine motor and eye-hand coordination are used in turning the cards over and also in setting the game up in an orderly fashion.

Chapter XI

MEMO
Skill List

Auditory skills
>auditory reception
>auditory association
auditory sequential
memory
auditory closure
>auditory manual expression
auditory sound blending
>auditory vocabulary
auditory word attack
>auditory discrimination
>auditory perception
>auditory memory

Visual skills
>visual reception
>visual association
visual sequential
memory
visual closure
visual grammatic
closure
>visual discrimination
>visual perception
>visual memory
visual eye tracking
>visual eye-hand coordination
>visual sorting
figure ground

Motor skills
>fine motor
gross motor
sensory motor

Directional skills
>right and left
>up and down
>laterality
>directionality

Modality
>modality
>cross modality

Attention
>visual attention
auditory attention
>motor attention
>spatial attention

Educational Skills
tenses
phonics
spelling
sentence structure
arithmetic
prefixes
suffixes
plurals
vocabulary
general information
>thought process
development
>perceptual consistency
inner language process
>color discrimination
conceptual development
logical reasoning
numerical discrimination
expression
>differentiating
decoding
encoding
word attack
retrieval of information
sequencing
comprehension
perseveration
dictionary skills
mental agility
analysis
synthesis

Social skills
behavior
attitude
winning
losing
sharing
patience
tolerance
interactions
actions
reactions
consequences
appropriate conversation
self control
self esteem
impulsiveness
communication
>compulsiveness
social perception
social maturation
self concept

Memory skills
>short term memory
>sequential memory
>long term memory

Chapter XI
MEMORY MATCHDOWN

Memory, short term and visual, is the emphasis here. Clues or glimpses of colors, shapes, sizes and recall assist you but it is necessary to combine these with laterality and spatial concepts or you will come up miss matching the pairs. New strategies are available as you try to match the pictures. For example, remembering the nothern, right hand corner area: second card from the right or sixth card from the left: fifth card from the southern, right hand corner, or the second from the north, headed south -- you do get the point, do you not? Oops! Did I just see your opponent match the one that you were trying to remember?

MEMORY MATCHDOWN
Skill List

Auditory skills
>auditory reception
auditory association
auditory sequential
 memory
auditory closure
>auditory manual ex-
 pression
auditory sound blend-
 ing
auditory vocabulary
auditory word attack
auditory discrimina-
 tion
auditory perception
>auditory memory

Visual skills
>visual reception
>visual association
visual sequential
 memory
visual closure
visual grammatic
 closure
>visual discrimination
>visual perception
>visual memory
>visual eye tracking
>visual eye-hand coor-
 dination
>visual sorting
figure ground

Motor skills
>fine motor
gross motor
sensory motor

Directional skills
>right and left
>up and down
>laterality
>directionality

Modality
>modality
>cross modality

Attention
>visual attention
>auditory attention
>motor attention
>spatial attention

Educational Skills
tenses
phonics
spelling
sentence structure
arithmetic
prefixes
suffixes
plurals
vocabulary
>general information
>thought process
 development
>perceptual consistency
inner language process
>color discrimination
>conceptual develop-
 ment
>logical reasoning
numerical discrimina-
 tion
expression
>differentiating
>decoding
encoding
word attack
>retrieval of informa-
 tion
sequencing
comprehension
perseveration
dictionary skills
>mental agility
>analysis
synthesis

Social skills
behavior
attitude
winning
losing
sharing
patience
tolerance
interactions
actions
reactions
consequences
appropriate conversa-
 tion
self control
self esteem
impulsiveness
cmmunication
compulsiveness
social perception
social maturation
self concept

Memory skills
>short term memory
>sequential memory
>long term memory

MEMO - REMEMBER THE ANIMALS

Memo really tugs the short-term memory and indirectly touches the long term as it gets the visual memory integrated with a clue system that turns into strategy. This system of clues for remembering gets complex as your spatial, motor, directionality, laterality and numerous visual skills come into play. "Where was it", could be thought of as a new title for this game.

Animal Pairs and Animal Homes can both be played with these cards. Many other variations are possible for each of these games. This a marvelous family game for including the young children and it is a good skill builder for all ages. Thirty six matching sets are in the game. "Who remembers where the home of the horse is?" "No! Not the cage holding the bird again!" These comments and more are running constantly in the conversation. Soon everyone is as happy as a jack rabbit...no, that's a regular rabbit sometimes known as a (hair) hare! This game provides a grand opportunity for adding a few subtle extras as you play...homonyms, for example.

Chapter XI

MEMO - REMEMBER THE ANIMALS
Skill List

Auditory skills
>auditory reception
auditory association
auditory sequential
  memory
auditory closure
>auditory manual expression
auditory sound blending
auditory vocabulary
auditory word attack
auditory discrimination
auditory perception
>auditory memory

Visual skills
>visual reception
>visual association
>visual sequential
  memory
>visual closure
>visual grammatic
  closure
>visual discrimination
>visual perception
>visual memory
>visual eye tracking
>visual eye-hand coordination
>visual sorting
>figure ground

Motor skills
>fine motor
gross motor
>sensory motor

Directional skills
>right and left
>up and down
>laterality
>directionality

Modality
>modality
>cross modality

Attention
>visual attention
>auditory attention
>motor attention
>spatial attention

Educational Skills
tenses
phonics
spelling
sentence structure
arithmetic
prefixes
suffixes
plurals
vocabulary
>general information
>thought process
  development
>perceptual consistency
  inner language process
>color discrimination
  conceptual development
logical reasoning
numerical discrimination
>expression
>differentiating
decoding
encoding
word attack
>retrieval of information
sequencing
comprehension
>perseveration
dictionary skills
mental agility
analysis
synthesis

Social skills
behavior
attitude
winning
losing
sharing
patience
tolerance
interactions
actions
reactions
consequences
appropriate conversation
self control
self esteem
impulsiveness
communication
compulsiveness
social perception
social maturation
self concept

Memory skills
>short term memory
>sequential memory
>long term memory

Chapter XI

MONOPOLY

How do you name the skills of Monopoly,
when it's the game that has them all?
You can only attend a few,
located in your immediate recall!

MONOPOLY
Skill List

Auditory skills
>auditory reception
>auditory association
>auditory sequential memory
>auditory closure
>auditory manual expression
>auditory sound blending
>auditory vocabulary
>auditory word attack
>auditory discrimination
>auditory perception
>auditory memory

Visual skills
>visual reception
>visual association
>visual sequential memory
>visual closure
>visual grammatic closure
>visual discrimination
>visual perception
>visual memory
>visual eye tracking
>visual eye-hand coordination
>visual sorting
>figure ground

Motor skills
>fine motor
gross motor
>sensory motor

Directional skills
>right and left
>up and down
>laterality
>directionality

Modality
>modality
>cross modality

Attention
>visual attention
>auditory attention
>motor attention
>spatial attention

Educational Skills
>tenses
>phonics
>spelling
>sentence structure
>arithmetic
>prefixes
>suffixes
>plurals
>vocabulary
>general information
>thought process development
>perceptual consistency
>inner language process
>color discrimination
>conceptual development
>logical reasoning
>numerical discrimination
>expression
>differentiating
>decoding
>encoding
>word attack
>retrieval of information
>sequencing
>comprehension
>perseveration
>dictionary skills
>mental agility
>analysis
>synthesis

Social skills
behavior
attitude
winning
losing
sharing
patience
tolerance
interactions
actions
reactions
consequences
appropriate conversation
self control
self esteem
impulsiveness
communication
compulsiveness
social perception
social maturation
self concept

Memory skills
>short term memory
>sequential memory
>long term memory

Chapter XI

MOUSE TRAP

Mouse Trap is a unique game when compared to other board games. It can also be compared to setting a real mouse trap because many of the same skills are involved. Don't get your finger caught!! Becoming adept at fine motor skills prevents this torture. The game involves seeing and putting action into the sequencing process. This involves a number of senses and skills giving insurance for permanent learning. Mouse Trap correlates visual sorting of all the pieces that are to be put together along with visual directions given in words and pictures. Visual perception, visual, motor, and spatial attention, eye-hand coordination and sequencing are all put to great use in the building of the board and the mouse trap mechanism. This mechanism, much like a real mouse trap, shows action/reaction and as you play, the different action/reaction steps are seen and learned. Addition and subtraction are used in conjunction with strategy when you try to catch your opponent's mouse. The trick is to save your cheese, happy hunting.

MOUSE TRAP
Skill List

Auditory skills	Modality	Social skills

Auditory skills
>auditory reception
 auditory association
 auditory sequential
  memory
 auditory closure
>auditory manual ex-
  pression
 auditory sound blend-
  ing
 auditory vocabulary
 auditory word attack
 auditory discrimina-
  tion
 auditory perception
>auditory memory

Visual skills
>visual reception
 visual association
>visual sequential
  memory
 visual closure
 visual grammatic
  closure
 visual discrimination
>visual perception
>visual memory
>visual eye tracking
>visual eye-hand coor-
  dination
>visual sorting
>figure ground

Motor skills
>fine motor
 gross motor
>sensory motor

Directional skills
>right and left
>up and down
>laterality
>directionality

Modality
>modality
>cross modality

Attention
>visual attention
>auditory attention
>motor attention
>spatial attention

Educational Skills
 tenses
 phonics
 spelling
 sentence structure
>arithmetic
 prefixes
 suffixes
 plurals
 vocabulary
>general information
>thought process
  development
>perceptual consistency
 inner language process
>color discrimination
 conceptual develop-
  ment
>logical reasoning
 numerical discrimina-
  tion
>expression
 differentiating
 decoding
 encoding
 word attack
>retrieval of informa-
  tion
>sequencing
 comprehension
 perseveration
 dictionary skills
>mental agility
 analysis
 synthesis

Social skills
 behavior
 attitude
 winning
 losing
 sharing
 patience
 tolerance
 interactions
 actions
 reactions
 consequences
 appropriate conversa-
  tion
 self control
 self esteem
 impulsiveness
 communication
 compulsiveness
 social perception
 social maturation
 self concept

Memory skills
>short term memory
>sequential memory
>long term memory

Chapter XI

NUMBER AND QUALITY

Number and Quality is an interesting game. The top half of each card contains a number and the bottom half of each card contains a picture of different items. The two halves are different in quantity. The object is to interlock corresponding halves. You may locate matching items and numbers but still find that the missing possibility is that interlocking cannot occur. It happens, of course, because the two slots are not adaptable for a correct match.

Fun is yours while you build spatial, motor and visual skills. Coordinating these skills is the most difficult task. It is a great little game that is handy enough to carry anywhere. It can be played by many or by one.

Chapter XI

NUMBER AND QUALITY
Skill List

Auditory skills
auditory reception
auditory association
auditory sequential
  memory
auditory closure
auditory manual ex-
  pression
auditory sound blend-
  ing
auditory vocabulary
auditory word attack
auditory discrimina-
  tion
auditory perception
auditory memory

Visual skills
>visual reception
>visual association
>visual sequential
  memory
visual closure
visual grammatic
  closure
visual discrimination
>visual perception
>visual memory
>visual eye tracking
>visual eye-hand coor-
  dination
visual sorting
figure ground

Motor skills
>fine motor
gross motor
sensory motor

Directional skills
right and left
up and down
>laterality
>directionality

Modality
>modality
>cross modality

Attention
>visual attention
auditory attention
>motor attention
>spatial attention

Educational Skills
tenses
phonics
spelling
sentence structure
arithmetic
prefixes
suffixes
plurals
vocabulary
>general information
>thought process
  development
perceptual consistency
>inner language process
>color discrimination
conceptual develop-
  ment
logical reasoning
numerical discrimina-
  tion
expression
>differentiating
>decoding
encoding
word attack
retrieval of informa-
  tion
sequencing
comprehension
>perseveration
dictionary skills
>mental agility
analysis
synthesis

Social skills
behavior
attitude
winning
losing
sharing
patience
tolerance
interactions
actions
reactions
consequences
appropriate conversa-
  tion
self control
self esteem
impulsiveness
communication
compulsiveness
social perception
social maturation
self concept

Memory skills
>short term memory
sequential memory
>long term memory

175

NUMBER RINGS

Get ready to add, subtract, multiply and divide, now! To place all of your rings either in your corner or your opponent's, becomes more difficult with each roll of the dice.

When you learn to combine a little visual perception, reception and discrimination with-eye hand coordination, your brain is just beginning to comprehend the meaning of numerical manipulation. Yes, you use every possible number operation plus a dab of color coordination!

Strategy becomes just as good as your ability allows in deciding all that is to be done with the three numbers you roll. For example, if you roll a 2, 5 and 6 on your dice, you can consider:

$$2 \times 5 + 6 = 16 \quad 2 + 5 + 6 = 13 \quad 2 \times 6 + 5 = 17$$
$$6 \times 5 / 2 = 15 \quad 5 - 2 \times 6 = 18 \quad 2 \times 6 - 5 = 7$$

plus many other combinations! As you near the end of the game, your ability becomes quicker and sharper because your choices diminish in number.

The blocking, unblocking and getting out of the BONE YARD keeps a tight grip on your undivided attention. The many mathematical operations can be deepened into the use of square roots, powers or any other operational process that one's unique brain can imagine. Get your thinking cap on, it is time to prove your mathematical prowess and ingenuity!

NUMBER RINGS
Skill List

Auditory skills
auditory reception
auditory association
auditory sequential
memory
auditory closure
>auditory manual ex-
pression
auditory sound blend-
ing
auditory vocabulary
auditory word attack
auditory discrimination
auditory perception
auditory memory

Visual skills
>visual reception
visual association
visual sequential
memory
visual closure
visual grammatic
closure
>visual discrimination
visual perception
visual memory
>visual eye tracking
>visual eye-hand coor-
dination
visual sorting
figure ground

Motor skills
>fine motor
gross motor
sensory motor

Directional skills
>right and left
>up and down
>laterality
>directionality

Modality
>modality
cross modality

Attention
>visual attention
auditory attention
>motor attention
>spatial attention

Educational Skills
tenses
phonics
spelling
sentence structure
>arithmetic
prefixes
suffixes
plurals
vocabulary
general information
thought process
development
perceptual consistency
inner language process
>color discrimination
>conceptual develop-
ment
>logical reasoning
>numerical discrimina-
tion
expression
>differentiating
decoding
encoding
word attack
>retrieval of information
>sequencing
>comprehension
>perseveration
dictionary skills
>mental agility
>analysis
synthesis

Social skills
behavior
attitude
winning
losing
sharing
patience
tolerance
interactions
actions
reactions
consequences
appropriate conversa-
tion
self control
self esteem
impulsiveness
communication
compulsiveness
social perception
social maturation
self concept

Memory skills
>short term memory
>sequential memory
>long term memory

177

Chapter XI

OLD MAID

Who wants to be an old maid? No one that we have
played! This game offers skill practice in visual memory,
fine motor movement, matching, discrimination and perception. It also gives you that funny feeling inside of "being
cornered" or "being caught". (see glossary) A little mental
stress and anxiety are present as you try to rid your hand of
the "lady" without changing facial expressions.

This anxiety is just as noticeable when you select a
card from your opponent knowing that you may be getting
her! We must agree that pure chance plays a big part in this
game but you gain from learning to take the chance and
rework it if possible. After all, who wants to be caught
being the Old Maid?

OLD MAID
Skill List

<u>Auditory skills</u>
auditory reception
>auditory association
auditory sequential
memory
auditory closure
auditory manual ex-
pression
auditory sound blend-
ing
auditory vocabulary
>auditory word attack
auditory discrimina-
tion
>auditory perception
>auditory memory

<u>Visual skills</u>
visual reception
visual association
visual sequential
memory
visual closure
visual grammatic
closure
>visual discrimination
>visual perception
visual memory
visual eye tracking
>visual eye-hand coor-
dination
>visual sorting
figure ground

<u>Motor skills</u>
>fine motor
gross motor
>sensory motor

<u>Directional skills</u>
right and left
up and down
>laterality
>directionality

<u>Modality</u>
modality
>cross modality

<u>Attention</u>
>visual attention
>auditory attention
>motor attention
>spatial attention

<u>Educational Skills</u>
tenses
phonics
spelling
sentence structure
arithmetic
prefixes
suffixes
plurals
vocabulary
>general information
>thought process
development
>perceptual consistency
inner language process
color discrimination
conceptual develop-
ment
>logical reasoning
numerical discrimina-
tion
expression
differentiating
decoding
encoding
word attack
retrieval of informa-
tion
>sequencing
comprehension
>perseveration
dictionary skills
>mental agility
analysis
synthesis

<u>Social skills</u>
behavior
attitude
winning
losing
sharing
patience
tolerance
interactions
actions
reactions
consequences
appropriate conversa-
tion
self control
self esteem
impulsiveness
communication
compulsiveness
social perception
social maturation
self concept

<u>Memory skills</u>
>short term memory
sequential memory
long term memory

179

Chapter XI

O'NO 99

O'No 99 is a card game using visual perception and visual memory. This game also brings in auditory expression as you add and subtract the numbers orally each play. The better part of this game is the mental computation it requires as you climb toward the magic 99.

Sight vocabulary, color coordination plus visual and auditory attention are in evidence along with good practice in differentiating the numerical names for younger children, or for any of us who confuse numbers like 6, 9, 3, 5, and so forth. Even negative number meaning can be identified in this game. For example, if the score is zero and a minus ten is played, the score becomes a negative ten! Children begin to understand the meaning of positive and negative numbers which adds more meaning to their concept of the number line.

O'NO 99
Skill List

Auditory skills
>auditory reception
>auditory association
>auditory sequential
 memory
 auditory closure
>auditory manual ex-
 pression
 auditory sound blend-
 ing
 auditory vocabulary
 auditory word attack
 auditory discrimina-
 tion
>auditory perception
>auditory memory

Visual skills
>visual reception
>visual association
>visual sequential
 memory
 visual closure
 visual grammatic
 closure
>visual discrimination
>visual perception
>visual memory
>visual eye tracking
>visual eye-hand coor-
 dination
>visual sorting
 figure ground

Motor skills
>fine motor
 gross motor
 sensory motor

Directional skills
>right and left
 up and down
>laterality
>directionality

Modality
>modality
>cross modality

Attention
>visual attention
>auditory attention
>motor attention
>spatial attention

Educational Skills
 tenses
 phonics
 spelling
 sentence structure
 arithmetic
 prefixes
 suffixes
 plurals
>vocabulary
>general information
>thought process
 development
>perceptual consistency
>inner language process
>color discrimination
>conceptual develop-
 ment
>logical reasoning
 numerical discrimina-
 tion
 expression
>differentiating
>decoding
 encoding
 word attack
 retrieval of informa-
 tion
>sequencing
 comprehension
>perseveration
 dictionary skills
 mental agility
 analysis

synthesis

Social skills
 behavior
 attitude
 winning
 losing
 sharing
 patience
 tolerance
 interactions
 actions
 reactions
 consequences
 appropriate conversa-
 tion
 self control
 self esteem
 impulsiveness
 communication
 compulsiveness
 social perception
 social maturation
 self concept

Memory skills
>short term memory
 sequential memory
>long term memory

OPERATION

When the patient's nose lights up and he buzzes loudly, don't be alarmed. It will end by the time your nerves recover! Operation offers the finest of fine motor skill development. The object is to pick up a body part such as a funny bone or a broken heart but the catch is that you must do this without the tweezers touching the sides of the patient's body...unless, of course, batteries are dead. Eye-hand coordination, sensitivity of touch, and fine motor skills are superbly interwoven into this operation. Remember, his life is in your hands because you are the doctor. Visual, spatial, and motor attention are also necessary in the specialization of this surgery. Playing Operation requires a physical combination of muscle and nerve that surpasses the requirements of most games. (More could be written about this game but one of the authors was unable to control her nervous reaction to the buzzer. In fact, the tenseness might equal that of a shock treatment!)

Chapter XI

OPERATION
Skill List

Auditory skills
>auditory reception
>auditory association
auditory sequential
memory
auditory closure
auditory manual ex-
pression
auditory sound blend-
ing
auditory vocabulary
auditory word attack
>auditory discrimination
>auditory perception
>auditory memory

Visual skills
>visual reception
>visual association
visual sequential
memory
visual closure
visual grammatic
closure
>visual discrimination
>visual perception
>visual memory
visual eye tracking
>visual eye-hand coor-
dination
visual sorting
figure ground

Motor skills
>fine motor
gross motor
>sensory motor

Directional skills
right and left
>up and down
>laterality
directionality

Modality
>modality
>cross modality

Attention
>visual attention
>auditory attention
>motor attention
>spatial attention

Educational Skills
tenses
phonics
spelling
sentence structure
arithmetic
prefixes
suffixes
plurals
vocabulary
>general information
>thought process
development
>perceptual consistency
>inner language process
>color discrimination
conceptual develop-
ment
logical reasoning
numerical discrimina-
tion
expression
>differentiating
>decoding
encoding
word attack
>retrieval of informa-
tion
sequencing
comprehension
perseveration
>dictionary skills
mental agility
analysis
>synthesis

Social skills
behavior
attitude
winning
losing
sharing
patience
tolerance
interactions
actions
reactions
consequences
appropriate conversa-
tion
self control
self esteem
impulsiveness
communication
compulsiveness
social perception
social maturation
self concept

Memory skills
>short term memory
>sequential memory
long term memory

OTHELLO

Othello says, "Get your fine motor muscles moving", and we say, "Oh, Othello, is it time to flip?" Flipping these little black and white flat pieces is a marvelous workout for fine motor and eye-hand coordination. Othello also allows perception and strategy to become a well coordinated team. Laterality and directionality are constants along with visual skills, mental agility and deductive reasoning. Have fun and flip 'em fast! If your hand gets quicker than your opponent's eye, you have it made!

OTHELLO
Skill List

Auditory skills
auditory reception
auditory association
auditory sequential
  memory
auditory closure
auditory manual ex-
  pression
auditory sound blend-
  ing
auditory vocabulary
auditory word attack
auditory discrimina-
  tion
auditory perception
auditory memory

Visual skills
>visual reception
visual association
visual sequential
  memory
visual closure
visual grammatic
  closure
>visual discrimination
>visual perception
>visual memory
>visual eye tracking
>visual eye-hand coor-
  dination
>visual sorting
>figure ground

Motor skills
>fine motor
gross motor
sensory motor

Directional skills
>right and left
>up and down
>laterality
>directionality

Modality
modality
cross modality

Attention
>visual attention
auditory attention
>motor attention
>spatial attention

Educational Skills
tenses
phonics
spelling
sentence structure
arithmetic
prefixes
suffixes
plurals
vocabulary
general information
>thought process
  development
>perceptual consistency
inner language process
>color discrimination
conceptual develop-
  ment
>logical reasoning
numerical discrimina-
  tion
expression
>differentiating
decoding
encoding
word attack
>retrieval of informa-
  tion
>sequencing
comprehension
perseveration
dictionary skills
>mental agility
>analysis
>synthesis

Social skills
behavior
attitude
winning
losing
sharing
patience
tolerance
interactions
actions
reactions
consequences
appropriate conversa-
  tion
self control
self esteem
impulsiveness
cmmunication
compulsiveness
social perception
social maturation
self concept

Memory skills
>short term memory
>sequential memory
>long term memory

185

OUT OF CONTEXT

Out of Context is a game of pure joy and relaxation for high school, college and adult ages. The fun of decision making is at its peak when you are deciding which quote each of these famous people would have said! This game of "no stress, just guess" is as funny as the author intended the directions to be! (We thank him for directions that portray a marvelous sense of humor). Many auditory skills are included, especially those of memory, expression and association. Sensory and social skills are stacked high and long-term and short-term memory work overtime! All reading skills are interwoven along with face control as you try to read the quotes without laughing.

"Multiple guess" is always good practice for teenagers and young adults since they face so many tests of multiple choice. Out of Context offers the place for honing your skills through fun and thrills!

Chapter XI

OUT OF CONTEXT
Skill List

Auditory skills
>auditory reception
>auditory association
>auditory sequential
 memory
>auditory closure
>auditory manual ex-
 pression
>auditory sound blend-
 ing
>auditory vocabulary
>auditory word attack
>auditory discrimination
>auditory perception
>auditory memory

Visual skills
>visual reception
>visual association
>visual sequential
 memory
>visual closure
>visual grammatic
 closure
>visual discrimination
>visual perception
>visual memory
>visual eye tracking
>visual eye-hand coor-
 dination
>visual sorting
>figure ground

Motor skills
>fine motor
 gross motor
>sensory motor

Directional skills
>right and left
>up and down
 laterality
>directionality

Modality
>modality
>cross modality

Attention
>visual attention
>auditory attention
>motor attention
>spatial attention

Educational Skills
>tenses
 phonics
>spelling
>sentence structure
 arithmetic
 prefixes
 suffixes
 plurals
>vocabulary
>general information
>thought process
 development
 perceptual consistency
>inner language process
 color discrimination
>conceptual develop-
 ment
>logical reasoning
 numerical discrimina-
 tion
>expression
>differentiating
 decoding
 encoding
>word attack
>retrieval of informa-
 tion
 sequencing
>comprehension
>perseveration
 dictionary skills
>mental agility
>analysis
>synthesis

Social skills
 behavior
 attitude
 winning
 losing
 sharing
 patience
 tolerance
 interactions
 actions
 reactions
 consequences
 appropriate conversa-
 tion
 self control
 self esteem
 impulsiveness
 communication
 compulsiveness
 social perception
 social maturation
 self concept

Memory skills
>short term memory
>sequential memory
>long term memory

187

PASSWORD

Auditory skills come alive in Password as you give synonyms, homonyms, antonyms, analogies and other clues to awaken your partner' s word recognition skills. Many skills of association are used along with comprehension and concentration. Word retrieval is a necessity for all players, and it needs to be quick!

This is a tremendous game for vocabulary building. It also gives you an on-the-spot interchange with your partner. This is a valuable skill used in all phases of life. "Thinking on your feet" provides children with practice that assists them in becoming less shy and more assertive. This is a sure way to better self esteem.

Many test taking skills are imbedded in Password, and all children need to play. Password is a little difficult for most people because it requires such fast thinking. However, enough practice will allow the fear to diminish. It is time to play!

Chapter XI

PASSWORD
Skill List

Auditory skills
>auditory reception
>auditory association
>auditory sequential
memory
>auditory closure
>auditory manual ex-
pression
>auditory sound blend-
ing
>auditory vocabulary
>auditory word attack
>auditory discrimina-
tion
>auditory perception
>auditory memory

Visual skills
>visual reception
>visual association
>visual sequential
memory
>visual closure
>visual grammatic
closure
>visual discrimination
>visual perception
>visual memory
>visual eye tracking
visual eye-hand coor-
dination
visual sorting
figure ground

Motor skills
>fine motor
gross motor
sensory motor

Directional skills
right and left
up and down
laterality
directionality

Modality
>modality
>cross modality

Attention
>visual attention
>auditory attention
motor attention
spatial attention

Educational Skills
tenses
phonics
spelling
sentence structure
arithmetic
prefixes
suffixes
plurals
>vocabulary
>general information
thought process
development
perceptual consistency
inner language process
color discrimination
conceptual develop-
ment
>logical reasoning
numerical discrimina-
tion
>expression
differentiating
decoding
encoding
>word attack
>retrieval of informa-
tion
sequencing
comprehension
perseveration
dictionary skills
>mental agility
>analysis
synthesis

Social skills
behavior
attitude
winning
losing
sharing
patience
tolerance
interactions
actions
reactions
consequences
appropriate conversa-
tion
self control
self esteem
impulsiveness
communication
compulsiveness
social perception
social maturation
self concept

Memory skills
>short term memory
sequential memory
>long term memory

189

PICK UP STICKS

Pick Up Sticks is a return to the "good old days". It is also a return to the "good old skills". Pick Up Sticks is tops for eye-hand coordination, agility, balance, and handling a little stress. Directionality has a different angle as you lift these little sticks up, down, out from under and around!

Motor, spatial and visual attention provide you with a steady hand and sure eye. Much action and reaction come forward as you achieve or as you see a stick wiggle! These plastic sticks are not the same as the painted wooden ones of years gone by, but they are still great for coordinating both your hand and your eye!

PICK UP STICKS
Skill List

Auditory skills
  auditory reception
  auditory association
  auditory sequential
    memory
  auditory closure
  >auditory manual ex-
    pression
  auditory sound blend-
    ing
  auditory vocabulary
  auditory word attack
  auditory discrimina-
    tion
  auditory perception
  auditory memory

Visual skills
  >visual reception
  >visual association
  >visual sequential
    memory
  visual closure
  visual grammatic
    closure
  >visual discrimination
  >visual perception
  >visual memory
  >visual eye tracking
  >visual eye-hand coor-
    dination
  >visual sorting
  figure ground

Motor skills
  >fine motor
  gross motor
  >sensory motor

Directional skills
  right and left
  >up and down
  >laterality
  >directionality

Modality
  >modality
  >cross modality

Attention
  >visual attention
  auditory attention
  >motor attention
  >spatial attention

Educational Skills
  tenses
  phonics
  spelling
  sentence structure
  arithmetic
  prefixes
  suffixes
  plurals
  vocabulary
  >general information
  >thought process
    development
  >perceptual consistency
  inner language process
  >color discrimination
  conceptual develop-
    ment
  >logical reasoning
  numerical discrimina-
    tion
  expression
  >differentiating
  decoding
  encoding
  word attack
  retrieval of informa-
    tion
  sequencing
  >comprehension
  >perseveration
  dictionary skills
  >mental agility
  analysis
  synthesis

Social skills
  behavior
  attitude
  winning
  losing
  sharing
  patience
  tolerance
  interactions
  actions
  reactions
  consequences
  appropriate conversa-
    tion
  self control
  self esteem
  impulsiveness
  communication
  compulsiveness
  social perception
  social maturation
  self concept

Memory skills
  >short term memory
  sequential memory
  >long term memory

PICTIONARY

This game may cause a little stress, even for the visual learner. The object is for your teammate to draw a picture and for you to guess what word he is trying to communicate. This game offers a great new twist and an excellent opportunity in developing a sense of suggestiveness from pictures rather than adhering to one's more literal translations of things seen. It even includes the possibility of developing a person's ability to visualize.

The game provides many skills that are not found in any other game. For example, drawing pictures to represent words such as citizen, is a skill that we have not found in any other game! It is a great game for provoking and promoting thinking before SAT time rolls around for high school students. This game has all the qualifications for a good time. Your pictures may offer something to think and laugh about for years. Get your crayons ready to roll.

PICTIONARY
Skill List

Auditory skills
>auditory reception
>auditory association
>auditory sequential
memory
>auditory closure
>auditory manual ex-
pression
>auditory sound blend-
ing
>auditory vocabulary
>auditory word attack
>auditory discrimina-
tion
>auditory perception
>auditory memory

Visual skills
>visual reception
>visual association
>visual sequential
memory
>visual closure
>visual grammatic
closure
>visual discrimination
>visual perception
>visual memory
>visual eye tracking
>visual eye-hand coor-
dination
>visual sorting
>figure ground

Motor skills
>fine motor
gross motor
>sensory motor

Directional skills
>right and left
>up and down
>laterality
>directionality

Modality
>modality
>cross modality

Attention
>visual attention
>auditory attention
>motor attention
>spatial attention

Educational Skills
tenses
phonics
spelling
sentence structure
arithmetic
prefixes
suffixes
plurals
>vocabulary
>general information
>thought process
development
>perceptual consistency
>inner language process
color discrimination
>conceptual develop-
ment
>logical reasoning
numerical discrimina-
tion
>expression
>differentiating
>decoding
>encoding
>word attack
>retrieval of informa-
tion
sequencing
>comprehension
>perseveration
dictionary skills
>mental agility
>analysis

>synthesis

Social skills
behavior
attitude
winning
losing
sharing
patience
tolerance
interactions
actions
reactions
consequences
appropriate conversa-
tion
self control
self esteem
impulsiveness
communication
compulsiveness
social perception
social maturation
self concept

Memory skills
>short term memory
>sequential memory
>long term memory

RACK - O

The sequencing in Rack-o is a new game. The process becomes more difficult because of all the rules and regulations involved. This is important because it forces the mind to think of the sequencing process, as you are using numbers that are far apart or running from large to small. Not being able to move your cards around can almost drive you "whack-o", as you visually and mentally sequence your way through Rack-o.

RACK - O
Skill List

Auditory skills
>auditory reception
auditory association
>auditory sequential
memory
auditory closure
>auditory manual expression
auditory sound blending
auditory vocabulary
auditory word attack
auditory discrimination
auditory perception
>auditory memory

Visual skills
>visual reception
visual association
visual sequential
memory
visual closure
visual grammatic
closure
visual discrimination
>visual perception
visual memory
visual eye tracking
>visual eye-hand coordination
>visual sorting
figure ground

Motor skills
>fine motor
gross motor
sensory motor

Directional skills
right and left
up and down
>laterality
>directionality

Modality
modality
>cross modality

Attention
>visual attention
auditory attention
>motor attention
>spatial attention

Educational Skills
tenses
phonics
spelling
sentence structure
arithmetic
prefixes
suffixes
plurals
vocabulary
>general information
>thought process
development
>perceptual consistency
inner language process
color discrimination
>conceptual development
>logical reasoning
>numerical discrimination
>expression
>differentiating
decoding
encoding
word attack
>retrieval of information
>sequencing
>comprehension
>perseveration
dictionary skills
>mental agility
>analysis
>synthesis

Social skills
behavior
attitude
winning
losing
sharing
patience
tolerance
interactions
actions
reactions
consequences
appropriate conversation
self control
self esteem
impulsiveness
communication
compulsiveness
social perception
social maturation
self concept

Memory skills
>short term memory
>sequential memory
>long term memory

Chapter XI

ROOK

Rook is a marvelous card game involving many skills that can be played over a wide range of ages. Through colors, number sequencing and visual discrimination, the cards are sorted, arranged and played. Many of the auditory and sensory skills are present and in action through the interchange of building, calling trumps and playing. The game offers much in mathematical estimation. For example, counting, adding and subtracting are a constant focus. Rook gives the learner a marvelous chance to develop judgement and common sense. Many strategies can be tried and sorted, finally allowing good ones to be selected for use and poor ones to be discarded.

Educational and social skills are so prevalent in this game that you will add to your list for a long time. Watch out! The Rook is ready to take you!

ROOK
Skill List

Auditory skills	Modality	Social skills
>auditory reception	>modality	behavior

Auditory skills
>auditory reception
>auditory association
auditory sequential
  memory
auditory closure
>auditory manual ex-
  pression
auditory sound blend-
  ing
>auditory vocabulary
auditory word attack
>auditory discrimina-
  tion
>auditory perception
>auditory memory

Visual skills
>visual reception
>visual association
>visual sequential
  memory
visual closure
visual grammatic
  closure
>visual discrimination
>visual perception
>visual memory
>visual eye tracking
>visual eye-hand coor-
  dination
>visual sorting
figure ground

Motor skills
>fine motor
gross motor
>sensory motor

Directional skills
>right and left
up and down
laterality
>directionality

Modality
>modality
>cross modality

Attention
>visual attention
>auditory attention
>motor attention
>spatial attention

Educational Skills
tenses
phonics
spelling
sentence structure
>arithmetic
prefixes
suffixes
plurals
vocabulary
>general information
>thought process
  development
>perceptual consistency
>inner language process
>color discrimination
>conceptual develop-
  ment
>logical reasoning
>numerical discrimina-
  tion
>expression
>differentiating
decoding
encoding
word attack
>retrieval of informa-
  tion
>sequencing
>comprehension
>perseveration
dictionary skills
>mental agility
>analysis
>synthesis

Social skills
behavior
attitude
winning
losing
sharing
patience
tolerance
interactions
actions
reactions
consequences
appropriate conversa-
  tion
self control
self esteem
impulsiveness
communication
compulsiveness
social perception
social maturation
self concept

Memory skills
>short term memory
sequential memory
>long term memory

ROUND FOUR

Round Four really gives you a visual workout including: perception, attention, coordination, sequencing, sorting, discrimination and tracking skills. Directionality runs a close second as your eyes flit in every direction keeping a close check on your opponent's strategy while developing your own. Attention is at its peak in this game in the areas of visual, motor and spatial learning. In fact, if the players do not attend carefully to these areas, auditory attention comes into play. As you hear the circles fall on the table, you realize that you have just lost the game!

ROUND FOUR
Skill List

Auditory skills	Modality	Social skills
>auditory reception	>modality	behavior
auditory association	>cross modality	attitude
auditory sequential		winning
memory		losing
auditory closure	Attention	sharing
>auditory manual ex- pression	>visual attention >auditory attention	patience tolerance
auditory sound blend- ing	>motor attention >spatial attention	interactions actions
auditory vocabulary		reactions
auditory word attack	Educational Skills	consequences

auditory discrimina-
  tion
	tenses
	phonics
		appropriate conversa-
		  tion

>auditory perception	spelling	self control
>auditory memory	sentence structure	self esteem
	arithmetic	impulsiveness
Visual skills	prefixes	communication
>visual reception	suffixes	compulsiveness
>visual association	plurals	social perception
>visual sequential	vocabulary	social maturation
memory	>general information	self concept
>visual closure	>thought process	
visual grammatic	development	Memory skills
closure	>perceptual consistency	>short term memory
>visual discrimination	inner language process	>sequential memory
>visual perception	>color discrimination	>long term memory
>visual memory	>conceptual develop-	
>visual eye tracking	ment	

>visual eye-hand coor-
  dination
	>logical reasoning
	  numerical discrimina-	

>visual sorting	tion	
figure ground	>expression	
	>differentiating	
Motor skills	decoding	
>fine motor	encoding	
gross motor	word attack	
sensory motor	>retrieval of informa- tion	
	>sequencing	
Directional skills	>comprehension	
>right and left	>perseveration	
>up and down	dictionary skills	
>laterality	>mental agility	
>directionality	analysis	
	synthesis	

RSVP

RSVP begins its skill list with directionality since you are playing both sides of an upright board -- building words up and down. While your word is reading 'snips' on your side of the board, it is reading 'spins' on the other side. That is not too confusing, but wait until the player or team opposite of you is spelling 'erugif'. On your side, it really looks weird. On the players side, this strange word is 'figure'. We assume that this is the definition of real reading...reading backwards and forwards, plus vertical and horizontal. Give it a try.

Many skills are involved in spelling, sounding and blending these words as well as in adding endings, beginnings and changing tenses. All of your visual skills come forward quickly. Visual perception, reception, memory, closure, discrimination, and tracking are a big part of this game. Attention is really the name of the game. In fact, visual, auditory, motor and spatial attention run rampant in RSVP.

The old dictionary comes in mighty handy when your partner builds a word like, fexazzerk! It is time to challenge and check with Mr. Webster. RSVP is a fun game for two or for teams. Teams are another marvelous way of assisting your children in becoming better spellers in a happy group setting. Be careful, the children may teach you some new words.

CHAPTER XI

RSVP
Skill List

Auditory skills
>auditory reception
>auditory association
>auditory sequential
  memory
>auditory closure
  auditory manual ex-
  pression
>auditory sound blend-
  ing
>auditory vocabulary
>auditory word attack
>auditory discrimina-
  tion
>auditory perception
>auditory memory

Visual skills
>visual reception
>visual association
>visual sequential
  memory
>visual closure
  visual grammatic
  closure
>visual discrimination
>visual perception
>visual memory
>visual eye tracking
>visual eye-hand coor-
  dination
  visual sorting
  figure ground

Motor skills
>fine motor
  gross motor
  sensory motor

Directional skills
>right and left
  up and down
  laterality
>directionality

Modality
>modality
>cross modality

Attention
>visual attention
>auditory attention
>motor attention
>spatial attention

Educational Skills
>tenses
>phonics
>spelling
  sentence structure
  arithmetic
>prefixes
>suffixes
>plurals
>vocabulary
>general information
>thought process
  development
>perceptual consistency
>inner language process
  color discrimination
>conceptual develop-
  ment
>logical reasoning
  numerical discrimina-
  tion
>expression
>differentiating
>decoding
>encoding
>word attack
>retrieval of informa-
  tion
>sequencing
>comprehension
>perseveration
  dictionary skills
>mental agility
>analysis
>synthesis

Social skills
  behavior
  attitude
  winning
  losing
  sharing
  patience
  tolerance
  interactions
  actions
  reactions
  consequences
  appropriate conversa-
  tion
  self control
  self esteem
  impulsiveness
  communication
  compulsiveness
  social perception
  social maturation
  self concept

Memory skills
>short term memory
>sequential memory
>long term memory

RUMMIKUB

Arithmetic? Mathematics? No, it's the science of numbers! All children need to develop an understanding of numbers. In this game, you manipulate numbers through matching or sequencing while combining a little color coordination. Concentration is a requirement as the game unfolds. Rummikub is marvelous for tracking and for visual discrimination of color and numbers. Grouping, regrouping, sorting and resorting make your brain work overtime to develop new strategies in your short-term memory that are to be practiced and stored in long-term memory as permanent learning.

Mental alertness or mental awareness is the name of the game as you become involved in visual, spatial, and motor attention!! In addition to all of the above, it is fun to play Rummikub.

CHAPTER XI

RUMMIKUB
Skill List

Auditory skills
>auditory reception
 auditory association
>auditory sequential
 memory
 auditory closure
>auditory manual ex-
 pression
 auditory sound blend-
 ing
 auditory vocabulary
 auditory word attack
 auditory discrimina-
 tion
 auditory perception
>auditory memory

Visual skills
>visual reception
>visual association
>visual sequential
 memory
>visual closure
>visual grammatic
 closure
>visual discrimination
>visual perception
>visual memory
>visual eye tracking
>visual eye-hand coor-
 dination
>visual sorting
>figure ground

Motor skills
>fine motor
 gross motor
>sensory motor

Directional skills
>right and left
 up and down
 laterality
>directionality

Modality
>modality
>cross modality

Attention
>visual attention
>auditory attention
>motor attention
>spatial attention

Educational Skills
 tenses
 phonics
 spelling
 sentence structure
 arithmetic
 prefixes
 suffixes
 plurals
>vocabulary
>general information
>thought process
 development
>perceptual consistency
>inner language process
>color discrimination
>conceptual develop-
 ment
>logical reasoning
>numerical discrimina-
 tion
>expression
>differentiating
 decoding
 encoding
 word attack
>retrieval of informa-
 tion
>sequencing
>comprehension
>perseveration
 dictionary skills
>mental agility
>analysis
>synthesis

Social skills
 behavior
 attitude
 winning
 losing
 sharing
 patience
 tolerance
 interactions
 actions
 reactions
 consequences
 appropriate conversa-
 tion
 self control
 self esteem
 impulsiveness
 communication
 compulsiveness
 social perception
 social maturation
 self concept

Memory skills
>short term memory
>sequential memory
>long term memory

Chapter XI

RUMMY

This is another "old timer" that needs little explanation but it is a splendid card game for two or more people to play! Visual skills are always actively involved in card games and they are outstanding in Rummy. Careful visual attention is required along with careful mental planning, abstract reasoning and strategy development.

Wonderful number manipulation and arrangement is apparent for players of Rummy and matching colors, numbers, runs, etc., runs hand in hand. This is an easy game to pack for a trip and fun, fun, fun to play at home.

RUMMY
Skill List

Auditory skills
>auditory reception
auditory association
>auditory sequential memory
auditory closure
>auditory manual expression
auditory sound blending
auditory vocabulary
auditory word attack
auditory discrimination
>auditory perception
>auditory memory

Visual skills
>visual reception
>visual association
>visual sequential memory
>visual closure
visual grammatic closure
>visual discrimination
>visual perception
>visual memory
>visual eye tracking
>visual eye-hand coordination
>visual sorting
figure ground

Motor skills
>fine motor
gross motor
sensory motor

Directional skills
right and left
up and down
laterality
>directionality

Modality
>modality
cross modality

Attention
>visual attention
auditory attention
>motor attention
>spatial attention

Educational Skills
tenses
phonics
spelling
sentence structure
arithmetic
prefixes
suffixes
plurals
vocabulary
>general information
>thought process development
>perceptual consistency
inner language process
>color discrimination
>conceptual development
>logical reasoning
>numerical discrimination
>expression
>differentiating
>decoding
encoding
word attack
>retrieval of information
>sequencing
comprehension
perseveration
dictionary skills
>mental agility
>analysis
>synthesis

Social skills
behavior
attitude
winning
losing
sharing
patience
tolerance
interactions
actions
reactions
consequences
appropriate conversation
self control
self esteem
impulsiveness
communication
compulsiveness
social perception
social maturation
self concept

Memory skills
>short term memory
>sequential memory
>long term memory

Chapter XI

SCORE FOUR

Score Four is a fun game that can be played with two or more people. Fine motor and eye-hand coordination take the lead in skills for this game as they race with strategy. Every phase of attention settles in quickly or your opponent will stack four balls on a stick before you know it! Perception and spatial awareness become the name of the game as you get further involved in playing.

Watching up, down, back and forth, is hard enough, but adding four levels of this keep your eyes jumping! The final wipeout is when your short term memory slips and your opponent sneaks in with a diagonal win.

When you would like to see a child's coordination and fine motor skills improve in the writing fingers, nothing is better than Score Four. (It surely is an improvement over poking peas through a hole in the top of a baby food jar!)

The quickness of this game adds much interest for children and allows perspective to develop at early ages. It is also pure joy to sit and devise new strategies, keep a straight face and hope to "pull one over" on your opponent!

SCORE FOUR
Skill List

Auditory skills
> auditory reception
  auditory association
  auditory sequential
    memory
  auditory closure
> auditory manual ex-
    pression
  auditory sound blend-
    ing
  auditory vocabulary
  auditory word attack
  auditory discrimina-
    tion
> auditory perception
> auditory memory

Visual skills
> visual reception
> visual association
> visual sequential
    memory
  visual closure
  visual grammatic
    closure
> visual discrimination
> visual perception
> visual memory
> visual eye tracking
> visual eye-hand coor-
    dination
> visual sorting
> figure ground

Motor skills
> fine motor
  gross motor
  sensory motor

Directional skills
> right and left
> up and down
> laterality
> directionality

Modality
> modality
> cross modality

Attention
> visual attention
  auditory attention
> motor attention
> spatial attention

Educational Skills
  tenses
  phonics
  spelling
  sentence structure
  arithmetic
  prefixes
  suffixes
  plurals
  vocabulary
> general information
> thought process
    development
> perceptual consistency
  inner language process
> color discrimination
> conceptual develop-
    ment
> logical reasoning
> numerical discrimina-
    tion
  expression
> differentiating
  decoding
  encoding
  word attack
  retrieval of informa-
    tion
> sequencing
  comprehension
  perseveration
  dictionary skills
> mental agility
> analysis
> synthesis

Social skills
  behavior
  attitude
  winning
  losing
  sharing
  patience
  tolerance
  interactions
  actions
  reactions
  consequences
  appropriate conversa-
    tion
  self control
  self esteem
  impulsiveness
  communication
  compulsiveness
  social perception
  social maturation
  self concept

Memory skills
> short term memory
> sequential memory
> long term memory

Chapter XI

SCRABBLE

Scrabble is reliable;
known to be tried and true!
It allows your brain to think,
what else can your brain do???

CHAPTER XI

SCRABBLE
Skill List

Auditory skills
>auditory reception
>auditory association
>auditory sequential
  memory
>auditory closure
>auditory manual ex-
  pression
>auditory sound blend-
  ing
>auditory vocabulary
>auditory word attack
>auditory discrimina-
  tion
>auditory perception
>auditory memory

Visual skills
>visual reception
>visual association
>visual sequential
  memory
>visual closure
>visual grammatic
  closure
>visual discrimination
>visual perception
>visual memory
>visual eye tracking
>visual eye-hand coor-
  dination
>visual sorting
>figure ground

Motor skills
>fine motor
  gross motor
  sensory motor

Directional skills
>right and left
>up and down
>laterality
>directionality

Modality
>modality
>cross modality

Attention
>visual attention
>auditory attention
>motor attention
>spatial attention

Educational Skills
>tenses
>phonics
>spelling
>sentence structure
  arithmetic
>prefixes
>suffixes
>plurals
>vocabulary
>general information
>thought process
  development
>perceptual consistency
>inner language process
  color discrimination
  conceptual develop-
  ment
>logical reasoning
  numerical discrimina-
  tion
  expression
>differentiating
>decoding
  encoding
>word attack
>retrieval of informa-
  tion
>sequencing
>comprehension
>perseveration
>dictionary skills
  mental agility
>analysis
>synthesis

Social skills
behavior
attitude
winning
losing
sharing
patience
tolerance
interactions
actions
reactions
consequences
appropriate conversa-
  tion
self control
self esteem
impulsiveness
communication
compulsiveness
social perception
social maturation
self concept

Memory skills
>short term memory
>sequential memory
>long term memory

209

Chapter XI

SCRABBLE SENTENCE CUBES

Search and find words, pictures, upper and lower case letters and minute punctuation! Look up, down, left and right. Search...locate...compare...match...decide and win as you combine your auditory, visual and spatial attentions to complete the sentences in this game. The amount of visual sorting or discriminating seems a little overwhelming in the beginning but the difficulty decreases as the game progresses. Visual closure skills aid you in finally inserting each missing part.

Hundreds of separate little skills begin to cooperate and coordinate as you attack each word and each sentence. Tracking around this board gives your brain new exercise. Short and long-term memory are in action as you hold and relate information. This game forces you to plan ahead and build strategies in order to become the winner. In every game of Sentence Scrabble for Juniors, you are winning...winning a review of skills that may have been otherwise overlooked!

SCRABBLE SENTENCE CUBES
Skill List

Auditory skills
>auditory reception
>auditory association
>auditory sequential
 memory
>auditory closure
>auditory manual ex-
 pression
>auditory sound blend-
 ing
>auditory vocabulary
>auditory word attack
>auditory discrimina-
 tion
>auditory perception
>auditory memory

Visual skills
>visual reception
>visual association
>visual sequential
 memory
>visual closure
>visual grammatic
 closure
>visual discrimination
>visual perception
>visual memory
>visual eye tracking
>visual eye-hand coor-
 dination
>visual sorting
>figure ground

Motor skills
>fine motor
 gross motor
 sensory motor

Directional skills
>right and left
>up and down
 laterality
>directionality

Modality
>modality
>cross modality

Attention
>visual attention
>auditory attention
>motor attention
>spatial attention

Educational Skills
>tenses
>phonics
>spelling
>sentence structure
 arithmetic
>prefixes
>suffixes
>plurals
>vocabulary
>general information
>thought process
 development
>perceptual consistency
>inner language process
>color discrimination
>conceptual develop-
 ment
>logical reasoning
 numerical discrimina-
 tion
>expression
>differentiating
>decoding
>encoding
>word attack
>retrieval of informa-
 tion
>sequencing
>comprehension
>perseveration
>dictionary skills
>mental agility
>analysis
>synthesis

Social skills
 behavior
 attitude
 winning
 losing
 sharing
 patience
 tolerance
 interactions
 actions
 reactions
 consequences
 appropriate conversa-
 tion
 self control
 self esteem
 impulsiveness
 communication
 compulsiveness
 social perception
 social maturation
 self concept

Memory skills
>short term memory
>sequential memory
>long term memory

SENTENCE BUILDER

This is a box of words and punctuations that add up to the sum total of an activity box. Various educational ideas can be dealt with using these 224 little cards. Activities such as pairing -- homonyms, synonyms, antonyms; categorizing and classifying -- animals, furniture, colors, etc.; matching -- beginning word sounds with letters and beginning or ending sounds in words; structuring sentences -- the four different kinds or just simple ones, are easily practiced in this game.

Todd tried the last suggestion and after five minutes his sentences read as follows:

A red flower is soon orange.

A hen was across the street.

Laugh at me! (I did!)

CHAPTER XI

SENTENCE BUILDER
Skill List

Auditory skills
>auditory reception
>auditory association
>auditory sequential memory
>auditory closure
>auditory manual expression
>auditory sound blending
>auditory vocabulary
>auditory word attack
>auditory discrimination
>auditory perception
>auditory memory

Visual skills
>visual reception
>visual association
>visual sequential memory
>visual closure
>visual grammatic closure
>visual discrimination
>visual perception
>visual memory
>visual eye tracking
>visual eye-hand coordination
>visual sorting
>figure ground

Motor skills
>fine motor
gross motor
sensory motor

Directional skills
right and left
up and down
laterality
>directionality

Modality
>modality
cross modality

Attention
>visual attention
>auditory attention
>motor attention
>spatial attention

Educational Skills
>tenses
>phonics
>spelling
>sentence structure
arithmetic
>prefixes
>suffixes
>plurals
>vocabulary
>general information
thought process development
perceptual consistency
>inner language process
color discrimination
conceptual development
>logical reasoning
numerical discrimination
>expression
differentiating
>decoding
>encoding
word attack
retrieval of information
sequencing
comprehension
perseveration
dictionary skills
>mental agility
>analysis
>synthesis

Social skills
behavior
attitude
winning
losing
sharing
patience
tolerance
interactions
actions
reactions
consequences
appropriate conversation
self control
self esteem
impulsiveness
communication
compulsiveness
social perception
social maturation
self concept

Memory skills
>short term memory
>sequential memory
>long term memory

SENTENCE SCRABBLE FOR JUNIORS

Search and find words, pictures, upper and lower case letters and minute punctuation marks. Look up, down, left and right. Search...locate...compare...match...decide and win as you combine your auditory, visual and spatial attentions to complete the sentences in this game. The amount of visual sorting or discrimination is a little overwhelming as the game begins but the difficulty decreases as the game progresses. Visual closure skills aid you in finally inserting each missing part. Hundreds of separate little skills begin to cooperate and coordinate as you attack each word and each sentence. Tracking around this board gives your brain new exercise. Short and long-term memory are in action as you hold and relate information. This game forces you to plan ahead and build strategies in order to become the winner. In every game of Sentence Scrabble for Juniors, you are winning...winning a review of skills that may have been otherwise overlooked!

CHAPTER XI

SENTENCE SCRABBLE FOR JUNIORS
Skill List

Auditory skills
>auditory reception
>auditory association
>auditory sequential
  memory
>auditory closure
>auditory manual ex-
  pression
>auditory sound blend-
  ing
>auditory vocabulary
>auditory word attack
>auditory discrimina-
  tion
>auditory perception
>auditory memory

Visual skills
>visual reception
>visual association
>visual sequential
  memory
>visual closure
>visual grammatic
  closure
>visual discrimination
>visual perception
>visual memory
>visual eye tracking
>visual eye-hand coor-
  dination
>visual sorting
>figure ground

Motor skills
>fine motor
  gross motor
  sensory motor

Directional skills
>right and left
>up and down
>laterality
>directionality

Modality
>modality
>cross modality

Attention
>visual attention
>auditory attention
>motor attention
>spatial attention

Educational Skills
>tenses
>phonics
>spelling
>sentence structure
  arithmetic
>prefixes
>suffixes
>plurals
>vocabulary
>general information
>thought process
  development
>perceptual consistency
>inner language process
  color discrimination
>conceptual develop-
  ment
>logical reasoning
  numerical discrimina-
  tion
>expression
>differentiating
>decoding
>encoding
>word attack
>retrieval of informa-
  tion
>sequencing
>comprehension
>perseveration
  dictionary skills
>mental agility
>analysis
>synthesis

Social skills
  behavior
  attitude
  winning
  losing
  sharing
  patience
  tolerance
  interactions
  actions
  reactions
  consequences
  appropriate conversa-
    tion
  self control
  self esteem
  impulsiveness
  communication
  compulsiveness
  social perception
  social maturation
  self concept

Memory skills
>short term memory
>sequential memory
>long term memory

SHIFTI

Talk about new strategies, Shifti has some! Just as you get going on your path toward a new home, your path moves, and you are left out in the cold until you see stars again! Shifti is new, fun and simple, but deep enough for conceptual growth. We guarantee this little game to get your directionality in tune as you improve your ability to visually receive, perceive, associate, discriminate and coordinate. A great deal of visual and spatial attention is necessary along with memory to wiggle your way from one corner to the next.

Strategy is required in this game in order for to make your plays -- usually in a game you can fumble along in moves -- not this time! A little inner-sensory transfer comes in handy as you differentiate and sequence your progress through the mixture of symbols found in your travels through this ever changing maze.

Oops! The board is moving again! Maybe this game should have been called..."Moving On!

CHAPTER XI

SHIFTI
Skill List

Auditory skills	Modality	Social skills

Auditory skills
>auditory reception
>auditory association
auditory sequential
  memory
auditory closure
>auditory manual ex-
  pression
auditory sound blend-
  ing
auditory vocabulary
auditory word attack
auditory discrimina-
  tion
>auditory perception
auditory memory

Visual skills
>visual reception
>visual association
>visual sequential
  memory
>visual closure
>visual grammatic
  closure
>visual discrimination
>visual perception
>visual memory
>visual eye tracking
>visual eye-hand coor-
  dination
>visual sorting
>figure ground

Motor skills
>fine motor
gross motor
sensory motor

Directional skills
>right and left
>up and down
>laterality
>directionality

Modality
>modality
>cross modality

Attention
>visual attention
auditory attention
>motor attention
>spatial attention

Educational Skills
tenses
phonics
spelling
sentence structure
arithmetic
prefixes
suffixes
plurals
vocabulary
>general information
>thought process
  development
>perceptual consistency
>inner language process
>color discrimination
>conceptual develop-
  ment
>logical reasoning
numerical discrimina-
  tion
>expression
>differentiating
  decoding
  encoding
  word attack
>retrieval of informa-
  tion
>sequencing
  comprehension
>perseveration
dictionary skills
>mental agility
analysis
synthesis

Social skills
behavior
attitude
winning
losing
sharing
patience
tolerance
interactions
actions
reactions
consequences
appropriate conversa-
  tion
self control
self esteem
impulsiveness
communication
compulsiveness
social perception
social maturation
self concept

Memory skills
>short term memory
>sequential memory
long term memory

Chapter XI

SPILL & SPELL

Spilling and spelling is fun for small, medium and large size children of all ages. This game is great to pull out of the closet at any time. It is a strong builder of vocabulary, word recall and word attack skills as you manipulate the letters to spell words up and down and side to side. It involves much mental manipulation as you get into the required organization and spatial placement. The blending and re-blending of sounds and letters require the use of many phonetic skills. Also, attached to this game is every ounce of attention that you can muster to keep your opponent from slipping a wrong word by without your noticing it. This game can even be used with youngsters without the timer for the purpose of building skills. It is quick, easy and challenging to play Spill & Spell.

CHAPTER XI

SPILL & SPELL
Skill List

Auditory skills
>auditory reception
>auditory association
>auditory sequential
  memory
>auditory closure
>auditory manual ex-
  pression
>auditory sound blend-
  ing
>auditory vocabulary
>auditory word attack
>auditory discrimina-
  tion
>auditory perception
>auditory memory

Visual skills
>visual reception
>visual association
  visual sequential
  memory
  visual closure
  visual grammatic
  closure
>visual discrimination
>visual perception
>visual memory
>visual eye tracking
>visual eye-hand coor-
  dination
>visual sorting
>figure ground

Motor skills
>fine motor
  gross motor
  sensory motor

Directional skills
>right and left
>up and down
>laterality
>directionality

Modality
>modality
>cross modality

Attention
>visual attention
>auditory attention
>motor attention
>spatial attention

Educational Skills
>tenses
>phonics
>spelling
  sentence structure
>arithmetic
>prefixes
>suffixes
>plurals
>vocabulary
>general information
  thought process
  development
  perceptual consistency
>inner language process
  color discrimination
  conceptual develop-
  ment
>logical reasoning
  numerical discrimina-
  tion
  expression
  differentiating
>decoding
>encoding
>word attack
  retrieval of informa-
  tion
>sequencing
  comprehension
  perseveration
  dictionary skills
>mental agility
>analysis
>synthesis

Social skills
  behavior
  attitude
  winning
  losing
  sharing
  patience
  tolerance
  interactions
  actions
  reactions
  consequences
  appropriate conversa-
  tion
  self control
  self esteem
  impulsiveness
  communication
  compulsiveness
  social perception
  social maturation
  self concept

Memory skills
>short term memory
>sequential memory
>long term memory

219

STING

Sting? Stang? Stung? You feel all three of these sensations, (whether they are real words or not), when every player dumps his cards in front of you. This game is full of visual skills to be practiced. Strategy holds a prominent ranking as you vigorously try to move the cards around in front of someone else! Runs, sets, colors and numbers facilitate your skill practice in this funny little card game. Sting is a feeling that you feel often when cards begin shifting in your direction.

CHAPTER XI

STING
Skill List

Auditory skills
>auditory reception
 auditory association
 auditory sequential
  memory
 auditory closure
>auditory manual ex-
  pression
 auditory sound blend-
  ing
 auditory vocabulary
 auditory word attack
 auditory discrimina-
  tion
 auditory perception
>auditory memory

Visual skills
>visual reception
>visual association
>visual sequential
  memory
 visual closure
 visual grammatic
  closure
 visual discrimination
>visual perception
>visual memory
 visual eye tracking
>visual eye-hand coor-
  dination
 visual sorting
 figure ground

Motor skills
>fine motor
 gross motor
 sensory motor

Directional skills
>right and left
 up and down
 laterality
>directionality

Modality
>modality
 cross modality

Attention
>visual attention
>auditory attention
>motor attention
>spatial attention

Educational Skills
 tenses
 phonics
 spelling
 sentence structure
 arithmetic
 prefixes
 suffixes
 plurals
 vocabulary
>general information
>thought process
  development
>perceptual consistency
>inner language process
>color discrimination
>conceptual develop-
  ment
>logical reasoning
>numerical discrimina-
  tion
>expression
>differentiating
 decoding
 encoding
 word attack
>retrieval of informa-
  tion
 sequencing
>comprehension
 perseveration
 dictionary skills
>mental agility
 analysis
 synthesis

Social skills
 behavior
 attitude
 winning
 losing
 sharing
 patience
 tolerance
 interactions
 actions
 reactions
 consequences
 appropriate conversa-
  tion
 self control
 self esteem
 impulsiveness
 communication
 compulsiveness
 social perception
 social maturation
 self concept

Memory skills
>short term memory
>sequential memory
>long term memory

Chapter XI

STRATEGO

Stratego, like Chess, requires excellent strategy and tremendous thinking. Before this game even begins, you must set the playing pieces up to suit your mental strategy of play. Short-term memory and long-term memory are both relied upon heavily as one strives to remember the rank of each of his opponents pieces and where each one is located. Remembering the rank becomes vitally important as each piece is revealed in play.

This game is a great build-up for higher thinking strategies and manipulation. Don't get blown away while stepping on a land mine!

CHAPTER XI

STRATEGO
Skill List

Auditory skills
>auditory reception
auditory association
auditory sequential
memory
auditory closure
>auditory manual expression
auditory sound blending
auditory vocabulary
auditory word attack
auditory discrimination
auditory perception
>auditory memory

Visual skills
>visual reception
>visual association
>visual sequential
memory
visual closure
visual grammatic
closure
>visual discrimination
>visual perception
visual memory
visual eye tracking
>visual eye-hand coordination
>visual sorting
figure ground

Motor skills
>fine motor
gross motor
sensory motor

Directional skills
>right and left
up and down
>laterality
>directionality

Modality
modality
cross modality

Attention
>visual attention
auditory attention
>motor attention
>spatial attention

Educational Skills
tenses
phonics
spelling
sentence structure
arithmetic
prefixes
suffixes
plurals
vocabulary
>general information
>thought process
development
>perceptual consistency
inner language process
color discrimination
>conceptual development
>logical reasoning
numerical discrimination
expression
differentiating
decoding
encoding
word attack
retrieval of information
sequencing
>comprehension
perseveration
dictionary skills
>mental agility
>analysis

>synthesis

Social skills
behavior
attitude
winning
losing
sharing
patience
tolerance
interactions
actions
reactions
consequences
appropriate conversation
self control
self esteem
impulsiveness
communication
compulsiveness
social perception
social maturation
self concept

Memory skills
>short term memory
sequential memory
>long term memory

223

THE UNGAME

Sneaky! Thousands of social skills arise in The Ungame as you become involved in the spontaneity of "off the cuff" or "on your feet" thinking. Verbalizing "on the spot" gives you an opportunity to deal with your feelings, attitudes, behaviors, self-control and self-esteem in an honest way as you determine self realizations!

Big skills of expression, intonation, reading, remembering and conceptualizing become second priority in this game! You can practice these and hundreds of other skills without thinking much about them because the brain has you so busy figuring out who you are and who you are becoming. Do not be surprised if you end up thinking in a whole new way! Attention gets caught in the right places in Ungame.

THE UNGAME
Skill List

Auditory skills
>auditory reception
>auditory association
>auditory sequential
 memory
>auditory closure
>auditory manual ex-
 pression
>auditory sound blend-
 ing
>auditory vocabulary
>auditory word attack
>auditory discrimina-
 tion
>auditory perception
>auditory memory

Visual skills
>visual reception
>visual association
>visual sequential
 memory
>visual closure
>visual grammatic
 closure
>visual discrimination
>visual perception
>visual memory
>visual eye tracking
 visual eye-hand coor-
 dination
 visual sorting
 figure ground

Motor skills
 fine motor
 gross motor
>sensory motor

Directional skills
 right and left
 up and down
 laterality
 directionality

Modality
>modality
>cross modality

Attention
>visual attention
>auditory attention
 motor attention
 spatial attention

Educational Skills
 tenses
 phonics
 spelling
 sentence structure
 arithmetic
 prefixes
 suffixes
 plurals
 vocabulary
>general information
>thought process
 development
 perceptual consistency
>inner language process
 color discrimination
 conceptual develop-
 ment
>logical reasoning
 numerical discrimina-
 tion
>expression
 differentiating
 decoding
 encoding
 word attack
>retrieval of informa-
 tion
 sequencing
>comprehension
 perseveration
 dictionary skills
 mental agility
>analysis
 synthesis

Social skills
 behavior
 attitude
 winning
 losing
 sharing
 patience
 tolerance
 interactions
 actions
 reactions
 consequences
 appropriate conversa-
 tion
 self control
 self esteem
 impulsiveness
 communication
 compulsiveness
 social perception
 social maturation
 self concept

Memory skills
>short term memory
>sequential memory
>long term memory

225

THE WORLD'S GREATEST TRAVEL GAME

All ages are invited to get into this little treasure chest! Seven games are described for your traveling pleasure and you can create more as you mix and match the cubes. Word attack skills, reading skills, motor skills, spatial skills, visual skills, auditory skills and attention skills are prevalent in these games:

FIVE IN A ROW
RISE TO THE TOP
SINK TO THE BOTTOM
GO FOR POINTS
THE HANDICAPPER
ONE BLOCK AT A TIME
GET NASTY
COMPOSITE GAME

We mention the skills in clusters above because they are so numerous in this number of games. This package is compact and ready to be your traveling partner anywhere in the world that you may choose to go.

CHAPTER XI

THE WORLD'S GREATEST TRAVEL GAME
Skill List

Auditory skills
>auditory reception
>auditory association
auditory sequential
memory
auditory closure
auditory manual ex-
pression
auditory sound blend-
ing
auditory vocabulary
auditory word attack
>auditory discrimina-
tion
>auditory perception
>auditory memory

Visual skills
>visual reception
>visual association
>visual sequential
memory
>visual closure
>visual grammatic
closure
>visual discrimination
>visual perception
>visual memory
>visual eye tracking
>visual eye-hand coor-
dination
>visual sorting
>figure ground

Motor skills
>fine motor
gross motor
>sensory motor

Directional skills
right and left
up and down
>laterality
>directionality

Modality
>modality
cross modality

Attention
>visual attention
auditory attention
>motor attention
>spatial attention

Educational Skills
tenses
phonics
spelling
sentence structure
arithmetic
prefixes
suffixes
plurals
vocabulary
>general information
>thought process
development
>perceptual consistency
>inner language process
>color discrimination
conceptual develop-
ment
>logical reasoning
numerical discrimina-
tion
expression
>differentiating
decoding
encoding
word attack
>retrieval of informa-
tion
sequencing
>comprehension
>perseveration
dictionary skills
>mental agility
>analysis

>synthesis

Social skills
behavior
attitude
winning
losing
sharing
patience
tolerance
interactions
actions
reactions
consequences
appropriate conversa-
tion
self control
self esteem
impulsiveness
communication
compulsiveness
social perception
social maturation
self concept

Memory skills
>short term memory
>sequential memory
>long term memory

TIME FACTOR

Time Factor is a delightful little game for two. It keeps your eyes, brains and fingers moving! Visual discrimination, sorting, association and motor memory combine into some skillful processing if you win this one. Spatial strategies and color coordination are a must. When your opponent keeps a straight face, anything can happen. The time factor may catch you if your opponent does not.

Time Factor is another good game to play when you have a short amount of time for playing. It is a great game for the waiting room since you never know how long you may be waiting.

TIME FACTOR
Skill List

Auditory skills
>auditory reception
auditory association
auditory sequential
memory
auditory closure
>auditory manual expression
auditory sound blending
auditory vocabulary
auditory word attack
auditory discrimination
auditory perception
auditory memory

Visual skills
>visual reception
visual association
visual sequential
memory
visual closure
visual grammatic
closure
visual discrimination
visual perception
>visual memory
visual eye tracking
>visual eye-hand coordination
>visual sorting
figure ground

Motor skills
>fine motor
gross motor
sensory motor

Directional skills
right and left
>up and down
>laterality
>directionality

Modality
>modality
>cross modality

Attention
>visual attention
auditory attention
>motor attention
>spatial attention

Educational Skills
tenses
phonics
spelling
sentence structure
arithmetic
prefixes
suffixes
plurals
vocabulary
>general information
thought process
development
perceptual consistency
inner language process
>color discrimination
>conceptual development
>logical reasoning
numerical discrimination
expression
>differentiating
decoding
encoding
word attack
>retrieval of information
>sequencing
comprehension
>perseveration
dictionary skills
>mental agility
analysis
synthesis

Social skills
behavior
attitude
winning
losing
sharing
patience
tolerance
interactions
actions
reactions
consequences
appropriate conversation
self control
self esteem
impulsiveness
communication
compulsiveness
social perception
social maturation
self concept

Memory skills
>short term memory
>sequential memory
>long term memory

TRI-OMINOES

Wow! What a mind boggler this game is as it forces you to keep your eyes tracking around hexagons and down lines, while searching inside and outside all of the strange shapes that are being constructed as play continues. Tracking for a matching set of numbers and adding points keeps your eyes and mind busy, but that is not all. The word, directionality, needs re-defining for this game! Visual attention, perception, closure, and association all coordinate and blend to give you visual memory. Tri-Ominoes is a marvelous game for removing transpositions and/or reversals of numbers.

CHAPTER XI

TRI - OMINOES
Skill List

Auditory skills
>auditory reception
auditory association
auditory sequential
  memory
auditory closure
>auditory manual ex-
  pression
auditory sound blend-
  ing
auditory vocabulary
auditory word attack
auditory discrimina-
  tion
auditory perception
auditory memory

Visual skills
>visual reception
>visual association
>visual sequential
  memory
>visual closure
visual grammatic
  closure
>visual discrimination
>visual perception
>visual memory
>visual eye tracking
visual eye-hand coor-
  dination
>visual sorting
>figure ground

Motor skills
>fine motor
gross motor
sensory motor

Directional skills
>right and left
>up and down
>laterality
>directionality

Modality
>modality
>cross modality

Attention
>visual attention
auditory attention
>motor attention
>spatial attention

Educational Skills
tenses
phonics
spelling
sentence structure
>arithmetic
prefixes
suffixes
plurals
vocabulary
>general information
>thought process
  development
>perceptual consistency
inner language process
color discrimination
>conceptual develop-
  ment
>logical reasoning
>numerical discrimina-
  tion
expression
>differentiating
decoding
encoding
word attack
>retrieval of informa-
  tion
>sequencing
>comprehension
>perseveration
dictionary skills
>mental agility
>analysis
synthesis

Social skills
behavior
attitude
winning
losing
sharing
patience
tolerance
interactions
actions
reactions
consequences
appropriate conversa-
  tion
self control
self esteem
impulsiveness
communication
compulsiveness
social perception
social maturation
self concept

Memory skills
>short term memory
sequential memory
>long term memory

TRIPOLEY

The chips are good counting pieces, especially if you are stacking them successfully on your side. This is a fun game for family and friends because it moves quickly and holds attention consistently. Visual perception, visual memory and visual sequential memory are being practiced continually but they are inadequate unless you have strategy or luck in your corner! Other games are described in the directions of Tripoley. Each game is strong in the development of visual skills and mental manipulation of colors, suits, runs, flushes, straights, pairs, full houses and sometimes four of a kind!

TRIPOLEY
Skill List

Auditory skills
>auditory reception
auditory association
auditory sequential memory
auditory closure
>auditory manual expression
auditory sound blending
>auditory vocabulary
auditory word attack
auditory discrimination
>auditory perception
>auditory memory

Visual skills
>visual reception
>visual association
>visual sequential memory
visual closure
visual grammatic closure
>visual discrimination
>visual perception
>visual memory
>visual eye tracking
>visual eye-hand coordination
>visual sorting
figure ground

Motor skills
>fine motor
gross motor
sensory motor

Directional skills
>right and left
up and down
laterality
>directionality

Modality
>modality
cross modality

Attention
>visual attention
>auditory attention
>motor attention
>spatial attention

Educational Skills
tenses
phonics
spelling
sentence structure
arithmetic
prefixes
suffixes
plurals
vocabulary
>general information
>thought process development
>perceptual consistency
>inner language process
>color discrimination
>conceptual development
>logical reasoning
>numerical discrimination
>expression
>differentiating
>decoding
>encoding
word attack
retrieval of information
>sequencing
>comprehension
>perseveration
dictionary skills
>mental agility
>analysis

>synthesis

Social skills
behavior
attitude
winning
losing
sharing
patience
tolerance
interactions
actions
reactions
consequences
appropriate conversation
self control
self esteem
impulsiveness
communication
compulsiveness
social perception
social maturation
self concept

Memory skills
>short term memory
>sequential memory
>long term memory

UNO

Uno becomes "oooooh, no!" as you play! Your opponent is constantly putting a card down to improve your reading skills! Believe me, you learn to read fast when you see words like "skip, reverse, draw two or draw four!" You are also reading numbers in addition to matching them to other numbers, colors and words. Fine motor skills, eye tracking, auditory expression, visual perception, reception, sorting and discrimination skills are all involved in the playing of Uno. Your strategies are always developing according to the cards that you hold in your hand. Much mental alertness including visual and auditory attention are required to keep you from saying, "Ooooh, No" rather than Uno!

CHAPTER XI

UNO
Skill List

Auditory skills
>auditory reception
auditory association
auditory sequential
memory
auditory closure
>auditory manual ex-
pression
auditory sound blend-
ing
auditory vocabulary
>auditory word attack
auditory discrimina-
tion
>auditory perception
auditory memory

Visual skills
>visual reception
>visual association
>visual sequential
memory
visual closure
visual grammatic
closure
visual discrimination
>visual perception
>visual memory
>visual eye tracking
>visual eye-hand coor-
dination
>visual sorting
figure ground

Motor skills
>fine motor
gross motor
sensory motor

Directional skills
>right and left
up and down
>laterality
>directionality

Modality
>modality
>cross modality

Attention
>visual attention
>auditory attention
>motor attention
>spatial attention

Educational Skills
tenses
phonics
spelling
sentence structure
arithmetic
prefixes
suffixes
plurals
vocabulary
>general information
>thought process
development
>perceptual consistency
inner language process
>color discrimination
conceptual develop-
ment
>logical reasoning
>numerical discrimina-
tion
expression
>differentiating
decoding
encoding
word attack
>retrieval of informa-
tion
>sequencing
>comprehension
perseveration
dictionary skills
mental agility
analysis
synthesis

Social skills
behavior
attitude
winning
losing
sharing
patience
tolerance
interactions
actions
reactions
consequences
appropriate conversa-
tion
self control
self esteem
impulsiveness
communication
compulsiveness
social perception
social maturation
self concept

Memory skills
>short term memory
>sequential memory
>long term memory

UNO-DOMINOS

For a different twist of Uno and a different twist of Dominoes, UNO-Dominos is the answer. Combining the two games has made a new game with more options to play. The game uses a great deal of visual memory in remembering where and how to play your different tiles and the different possibilities. All of the tiles have different numbers, colors and words which lead the player into visual discrimination of the tiles and into classifying and sorting them into different categories. In viewing all of the pieces on the table, tracking and directionality skills are used before a strategy can even be developed. Visual, spatial and motor attention skills are practiced as you place your pieces and watch as others play. Reading and understanding word directions are also used in this game. The words that are used on these tiles are so often repeated that they soon become sight vocabulary words.

CHAPTER XI

UNO DOMINOES
Skill List

Auditory skills
>auditory reception
auditory association
auditory sequential
memory
auditory closure
auditory manual ex-
pression
>auditory sound blend-
ing
auditory vocabulary
>auditory word attack
auditory discrimina-
tion
auditory perception
>auditory memory

Visual skills
>visual reception
visual association
>visual sequential
memory
visual closure
visual grammatic
closure
>visual discrimination
>visual perception
>visual memory
>visual eye tracking
>visual eye-hand coor-
dination
>visual sorting
figure ground

Motor skills
>fine motor
gross motor
sensory motor

Directional skills
>right and left
up and down
>laterality
>directionality

Modality
>modality
>cross modality

Attention
>visual attention
auditory attention
>motor attention
>spatial attention

Educational Skills
tenses
phonics
spelling
sentence structure
arithmetic
prefixes
suffixes
plurals
vocabulary
general information
>thought process
development
>perceptual consistency
inner language process
>color discrimination
>conceptual develop-
ment
>logical reasoning
>numerical discrimina-
tion
>expression
>differentiating
decoding
encoding
word attack
>retrieval of informa-
tion
sequencing
comprehension
perseveration
dictionary skills
mental agility
analysis
>synthesis

Social skills
behavior
attitude
winning
losing
sharing
patience
tolerance
interactions
actions
reactions
consequences
appropriate conversa-
tion
self control
self esteem
impulsiveness
communication
compulsiveness
social perception
social maturation
self concept

Memory skills
>short term memory
sequential memory
>long term memory

UNO WILD TILES

In playing Uno Wild Tiles a number of skills are being practiced. The game brings forth many visual skills that are used continuously. These include visual reception, visual association, visual discrimination, visual perception, visual tracking and visual attention. Uno Wild Tiles use spatial and motor attention along with eye-hand coordination and other fine motor skills. Directionality and laterality are skills used throughout the game in deciding the direction for each piece to be played. In making the decision of which piece should be played, a player begins to use strategy. He uses color discrimination and numerical discrimination in choosing his tiles. All of these skills add up to a good game that helps develop a variety of visual skills and begins simple strategy planning.

UNO WILD TILES
Skill List

Auditory skills
>auditory reception
auditory association
auditory sequential
memory
auditory closure
>auditory manual ex-
pression
auditory sound blend-
ing
auditory vocabulary
auditory word attack
>auditory discrimina-
tion
>auditory perception
>auditory memory

Visual skills
>visual reception
>visual association
visual sequential
memory
visual closure
visual grammatic
closure
>visual discrimination
>visual perception
>visual memory
>visual eye tracking
>visual eye-hand coor-
dination
>visual sorting
figure ground

Motor skills
>fine motor
gross motor
sensory motor

Directional skills
right and left
up and down
laterality
>directionality

Modality
>modality
cross modality

Attention
>visual attention
auditory attention
>motor attention
>spatial attention

Educational Skills
tenses
phonics
spelling
sentence structure
arithmetic
prefixes
suffixes
plurals
vocabulary
>general information
>thought process
development
>perceptual consistency
>inner language process
>color discrimination
>conceptual develop-
ment
>logical reasoning
>numerical discrimina-
tion
>expression
>differentiating
decoding
encoding
word attack
>retrieval of informa-
tion
sequencing
>comprehension
>perseveration
dictionary skills
>mental agility
>analysis

>synthesis

Social skills
behavior
attitude
winning
losing
sharing
patience
tolerance
interactions
actions
reactions
consequences
appropriate conversa-
tion
self control
self esteem
impulsiveness
communication
compulsiveness
social perception
social maturation
self concept

Memory skills
>short term memory
>sequential memory
>long term memory

Chapter XI

UPPER HAND

Talk about directions, these are much easier to follow if you already play Bridge. Fun is available for two, three or four players as you attack this "GRAND SLAM WORD GAME"! Directionality begins with north, east, south and west and it moves in the direction of "tricks"!

The contract idea is another good one because the process of negotiation is a marvelous skill for children to learn and it is not available in many games. This game comes with a glossary covering the basic terms of the game so learning in-depth begins immediately as you use all of your word attack and reading skills. Visual, auditory, educational, social, motor, spatial and common sense, skills are needed for this game. When you get the Upper Hand, give your memory an A plus.

Upper Hand is a marvelous game offering fun and challenge in every trick! Sit back, relax a little, because to win you must remain alert.

CHAPTER XI

UPPER HAND
Skill List

Auditory skills
>auditory reception
>auditory association
>auditory sequential
  memory
>auditory closure
>auditory manual ex-
  pression
>auditory sound blend-
  ing
>auditory vocabulary
  auditory word attack
>auditory discrimina-
  tion
>auditory perception
>auditory memory

Visual skills
>visual reception
>visual association
>visual sequential
  memory
>visual closure
>visual grammatic
  closure
>visual discrimination
>visual perception
>visual memory
>visual eye tracking
>visual eye-hand coor-
  dination
>visual sorting
>figure ground

Motor skills
>fine motor
  gross motor
  sensory motor

Directional skills
>right and left
>up and down
>laterality
>directionality

Modality
>modality
>cross modality

Attention
>visual attention
>auditory attention
>motor attention
>spatial attention

Educational Skills
  tenses
  phonics
  spelling
>sentence structure
  arithmetic
  prefixes
  suffixes
  plurals
>vocabulary
>general information
>thought process
  development
>perceptual consistency
>inner language process
  color discrimination
>conceptual develop-
  ment
>logical reasoning
  numerical discrimina-
  tion
  expression
>differentiating
>decoding
>encoding
>word attack
>retrieval of informa-
  tion
>sequencing
>comprehension
>perseveration
>dictionary skills
>mental agility
>analysis

>synthesis

Social skills
  behavior
  attitude
  winning
  losing
  sharing
  patience
  tolerance
  interactions
  actions
  reactions
  consequences
  appropriate conversa-
    tion
  self control
  self esteem
  impulsiveness
  communication
  compulsiveness
  social perception
  social maturation
  self concept

Memory skills
>short term memory
>sequential memory
>long term memory

Chapter XI

UPWORDS

What will they think of next? Words going up?? Words are running across, forward, up, out, down, over, under, sideways and skyward! How is this for directionality? laterality? Simultaneously, you are pulling on the old word attack skills like crazy. This three dimensional game is tremendous for spelling skills and reading skills as you "spell out, stack up and score high"!

All ages can play as you mentally scrounge around for new sounds and blends to change a word that is on the board or to make a new one of your very own. Either way, forming new words is marvelous for learning. You will get the hang of "upping" the letters by and by, as you stack them higher and higher, heading toward the sky!

UPWORDS
Skill List

Auditory skills
>auditory reception
>auditory association
>auditory sequential
  memory
>auditory closure
>auditory manual ex-
  pression
>auditory sound blend-
  ing
>auditory vocabulary
>auditory word attack
>auditory discrimina-
  tion
>auditory perception
>auditory memory

Visual skills
>visual reception
>visual association
>visual sequential
  memory
>visual closure
>visual grammatic
  closure
>visual discrimination
>visual perception
>visual memory
>visual eye tracking
>visual eye-hand coor-
  dination
>visual sorting
>figure ground

Motor skills
>fine motor
  gross motor
>sensory motor

Directional skills
>right and left
>up and down
>laterality
>directionality

Modality
>modality
>cross modality

Attention
>visual attention
>auditory attention
>motor attention
>spatial attention

Educational Skills
>tenses
>phonics
>spelling
  sentence structure
  arithmetic
>prefixes
>suffixes
>plurals
>vocabulary
>general information
>thought process
  development
  perceptual consistency
>inner language process
  color discrimination
>conceptual develop-
  ment
>logical reasoning
  numerical discrimina-
  tion
>expression
>differentiating
>decoding
>encoding
>word attack
>retrieval of informa-
  tion
>sequencing
>comprehension
>perseveration
>dictionary skills
>mental agility
>analysis

>synthesis

Social skills
  behavior
  attitude
  winning
  losing
  sharing
  patience
  tolerance
  interactions
  actions
  reactions
  consequences
  appropriate conversa-
    tion
  self control
  self esteem
  impulsiveness
  communication
  compulsiveness
  social perception
  social maturation
  self concept

Memory skills
>short term memory
>sequential memory
>long term memory

WHERE IS IT?

These games are suggested for ages three to seven and they provide good educational skills for children. Several different boards and games are included in this little box. These can be played alone or with others. Skills like directionality, matching pairs, visual and auditory learning are actively involved in these games. For example, left and right positions always need much practice. Where Is It provides this in a very pleasant way!

CHAPTER XI

WHERE IS IT?
Skill List

Auditory skills
> auditory reception
> auditory association
> auditory sequential memory
> auditory closure
> auditory manual expression
> auditory sound blending
> auditory vocabulary
> auditory word attack
> auditory discrimination
> auditory perception
> auditory memory

Visual skills
> visual reception
> visual association
> visual sequential memory
> visual closure
> visual grammatic closure
> visual discrimination
> visual perception
> visual memory
> visual eye tracking
> visual eye-hand coordination
> visual sorting
> figure ground

Motor skills
> fine motor
gross motor
sensory motor

Directional skills
> right and left
> up and down
> laterality
> directionality

Modality
> modality
> cross modality

Attention
> visual attention
auditory attention
> motor attention
> spatial attention

Educational Skills
tenses
phonics
spelling
> sentence structure
arithmetic
prefixes
suffixes
plurals
vocabulary
general information
thought process development
perceptual consistency
inner language process
> color discrimination
conceptual development
> logical reasoning
numerical discrimination
> expression
> differentiating
> decoding
> encoding
word attack
> retrieval of information
> sequencing
> comprehension
perseveration
dictionary skills
> mental agility
analysis

synthesis

Social skills
behavior
attitude
winning
losing
sharing
patience
tolerance
interactions
actions
reactions
consequences
appropriate conversation
self control
self esteem
impulsiveness
communication
compulsiveness
social perception
social maturation
self concept

Memory skills
> short term memory
> sequential memory
> long term memory

245

Chapter XI

WORD MASTER MIND

Without a doubt, Word Master Mind provides the most difficult route to a four letter word that your authors have ever found! Spelling is one thing, BUT un-spelling with strategies is another! This, is another mind boggler that includes all of the basic skills of word attack. You also use all of your skills of logic and attention! This is an extraordinary game for practicing deductive reasoning and conceptualization.

CHAPTER XI

WORD MASTER MIND
Skill List

Auditory skills
>auditory reception
>auditory association
>auditory sequential
  memory
>auditory closure
>auditory manual ex-
  pression
>auditory sound blend-
  ing
>auditory vocabulary
>auditory word attack
>auditory discrimina-
  tion
>auditory perception
>auditory memory

Visual skills
>visual reception
>visual association
>visual sequential
  memory
>visual closure
>visual grammatic
  closure
>visual discrimination
>visual perception
>visual memory
>visual eye tracking
>visual eye-hand coor-
  dination
>visual sorting
>figure ground

Motor skills
  fine motor
  gross motor
  sensory motor

Directional skills
  right and left
  up and down
  laterality
  directionality

Modality
  modality
  cross modality

Attention
>visual attention
>auditory attention
>motor attention
>spatial attention

Educational Skills
  tenses
>phonics
>spelling
  sentence structure
  arithmetic
>prefixes
>suffixes
>plurals
>vocabulary
>general information
>thought process
  development
>perceptual consistency
>inner language process
>color discrimination
>conceptual develop-
  ment
>logical reasoning
  numerical discrimina-
  tion
>expression
>differentiating
>decoding
>encoding
>word attack
>retrieval of informa-
  tion
>sequencing
>comprehension
>perseveration
  dictionary skills
>mental agility
>analysis

>synthesis

Social skills
  behavior
  attitude
  winning
  losing
  sharing
  patience
  tolerance
  interactions
  actions
  reactions
  consequences
  appropriate conversa-
  tion
  self control
  self esteem
  impulsiveness
  communication
  compulsiveness
  social perception
  social maturation
  self concept

Memory skills
>short term memory
>sequential memory
>long term memory

WORD YAHTZEE

It is difficult to imagine the fun and the skills to be found in seven letter dice, a timer, a cup and a score pad! Pleasure is steady as hundreds of skills unfold to be practiced and mastered. Any time you play word games all reading, phonic, visual and mental skills are being used; attention is being totally required for accurate deduction to occur; and all of these are even more prevalent when a timer is involved as it is in Word Yahtzee.

Scoring in this game gives marvelous mental math exercises to be performed. Just keep figuring with letters and with numbers...the big payoff comes when you realize how much better your skills are becoming after each game!

CHAPTER XI

WORD YAHTZEE
Skill List

Auditory skills
>auditory reception
>auditory association
>auditory sequential memory
>auditory closure
>auditory manual expression
>auditory sound blending
>auditory vocabulary
>auditory word attack
>auditory discrimination
>auditory perception
>auditory memory

Visual skills
>visual reception
>visual association
>visual sequential memory
>visual closure
>visual grammatic closure
>visual discrimination
>visual perception
>visual memory
>visual eye tracking
>visual eye-hand coordination
>visual sorting
>figure ground

Motor skills
>fine motor
gross motor
sensory motor

Directional skills
>right and left
>up and down
>laterality
>directionality

Modality
>modality
cross modality

Attention
>visual attention
>auditory attention
>motor attention
>spatial attention

Educational Skills
>tenses
>phonics
>spelling
>sentence structure
>arithmetic
>prefixes
>suffixes
>plurals
>vocabulary
>general information
>thought process development
>perceptual consistency
>inner language process
color discrimination
>conceptual development
>logical reasoning
>numerical discrimination
>expression
>differentiating
>decoding
>encoding
>word attack
>retrieval of information
>sequencing
>comprehension
>perseveration
>dictionary skills
>mental agility
>analysis

>synthesis

Social skills
behavior
attitude
winning
losing
sharing
patience
tolerance
interactions
actions
reactions
consequences
appropriate conversation
self control
self esteem
impulsiveness
communication
compulsiveness
social perception
social maturation
self concept

Memory skills
>short term memory
>sequential memory
>long term memory

249

Chapter XI

YAHTZEE

Roll the dice! Hope for a good roll! Straight flush, four of a kind, full house, straight, three of a kind, pairs, any of these goodies may transition into a score that really awakens your mental math skills. Visual skills blending with a bit of daring and counting gets into big numbers when scoring this game. This game is quick, interesting and fun for all ages. Actions and reactions are spontaneous as you await the outcome of each and every roll of the dice.

CHAPTER XI

YAHTZEE
Skill List

Auditory skills
>auditory reception
auditory association
auditory sequential
memory
auditory closure
auditory manual ex-
pression
auditory sound blend-
ing
>auditory vocabulary
auditory word attack
auditory discrimina-
tion
>auditory perception
>auditory memory

Visual skills
>visual reception
>visual association
>visual sequential
memory
visual closure
visual grammatic
closure
>visual discrimination
>visual perception
>visual memory
>visual eye tracking
>visual eye-hand coor-
dination
>visual sorting
figure ground

Motor skills
>fine motor
gross motor
sensory motor

Directional skills
right and left
>up and down
>laterality
>directionality

Modality
>modality
>cross modality

Attention
>visual attention
>auditory attention
>motor attention
>spatial attention

Educational Skills
tenses
phonics
spelling
sentence structure
>arithmetic
prefixes
suffixes
plurals
vocabulary
>general information
>thought process
development
>perceptual consistency
>inner language process
color discrimination
>conceptual develop-
ment
>logical reasoning
>numerical discrimina-
tion
expression
differentiating
decoding
encoding
word attack
>retrieval of informa-
tion
>sequencing
>comprehension
perseveration
dictionary skills
>mental agility
>analysis
>synthesis

Social skills
behavior
attitude
winning
losing
sharing
patience
tolerance
interactions
actions
reactions
consequences
appropriate conversa-
tion
self control
self esteem
impulsiveness
communication
compulsiveness
social perception
social maturation
self concept

Memory skills
>short term memory
>sequential memory
>long term memory

Chapter XI

YOUR AMERICA

This game is composed of outstanding historical and trivial questions about America! All reading skills are used as you quiz your opponent from the wide variety of questions provided for this game. During your turn all auditory skills are activated as you hear the questions and then pull on the old long term memory for the correct answer. This game is great for historical learning and the learning can be applied to any age or grade level. For example, "Which amendment created the income tax?", is one of the questions. (see glossary for answer under I.R.S.) We know this one will spark your interest! You do know about the I.R.S., do you not? Just thinking about its creation is mentally stimulating!

Auditory skills
>auditory reception
>auditory association
>auditory sequential
 memory
>auditory closure
>auditory manual ex-
 pression
>auditory sound blend-
 ing
>auditory vocabulary
>auditory word attack
>auditory discrimina-
 tion
>auditory perception
>auditory memory

Visual skills
>visual reception
>visual association
>visual sequential
 memory
>visual closure
>visual grammatic
 closure
>visual discrimination
>visual perception
>visual memory
>visual eye tracking
>visual eye-hand coor-
 dination
>visual sorting
>figure ground

Motor skills
>fine motor
>gross motor
>sensory motor

Directional skills
 right and left
 up and down
 laterality
 directionality

Modality
>modality
>cross modality

Attention
>visual attention
>auditory attention
 motor attention
 spatial attention

Educational Skills
>tenses
>phonics
>spelling
>sentence structure
>arithmetic
>prefixes
>suffixes
>plurals
>vocabulary
>general information
>thought process
 development
 perceptual consistency
>inner language
 process
 color discrimination
>conceptual develop-
 ment
>logical reasoning
 numerical discrimina-
 tion
>expression
 differentiating
>decoding
>encoding
>word attack
>retrieval of informa-
 tion
>sequencing
>comprehension
>perseveration
 dictionary skills
>mental agility
>analysis
>synthesis

Social skills
 behavior
 attitude
 winning
 losing
 sharing
 patience
 tolerance
 interactions
 actions
 reactions
 consequences
 appropriate conversa-
 tion
 self control
 self esteem
 impulsiveness
 communication
 compulsiveness
 social perception
 social maturation
 self concept

Memory skills
>short term memory
 sequential memory
>long term memory

To play is to learn! Playing is vital in developing your child's repertoire of experiences. Playing provides the same experiences for adults. Choose games for your family from our lists or from your own.

Everyone is born with a brain...is everyone born with a mind...or is it developed through the experiences one experiences?

Chapter XII

BECOMING WHOLE

We realize that we have only touched the surface with this book...that is the point! Now YOU can create all kinds of "fun and games" activities for your children and KNOW that you are doing the best thing possible for your family. Everyone can begin to relax and enjoy learning through play.

There are innumerable games on the market and all of them are skill builders. We have not discussed many of the educational games since they have already been labeled as educational. For young children you may want to use Light Up and Learn Sesame for improving visual and auditory discrimination. In fact, there is a Sesame game available for almost every skill and they are marvelous! Go Fish is another game that can be used to strengthen sight vocabulary. The Trivial games are also a set of games covering a wide range of skills for teenagers and adults. There is no end to the possibilities of learning through games! The point is, play! Give your child the freedom to get comfortable for learning! Have fun aiding your child in the process of BECOMING...WHOLE.

Points to remember!
- People's brains are as different as their faces.
- Anyone who can follow the directions of a new game can read and comprehend.
- Fear and impatience demagnetize your child; poise magnetizes.
- If you have trouble with directions, ask a child to help you.
- Self control and poise are developed in playing games.
- Games provide a controlled atmosphere that softly nudges one to learn.
- Games provide whole learning which is the acquisition of an entire task, skill, or concept at one time.

- The place for subtle and positive parental guidance is found in playing games.
- Strategies must be stored in the brain before new learning can be attached to them for permanent learning.
- Motivation arising from within is more stimulating.
- Attention spans are learned and developed.
- Young children are eager to learn; it is possible for their fun to continue forever...
- Games allow overlearning to be enjoyed.
- Test taking pressures are eased by playing through the pressures in games.
- Telling is not teaching; it is a turn off.
- It is easier to retain meaningful learning.
- Active learning is far better than passive learning.
- You can overload short term memory but you can not overload long term memory.
- A whole brain is smarter than its right or left side.
- Pride in accomplishment is felt when you make a good play...in a game.
- Winning or losing is acceptable when self-esteem is in tact.
- Losing is not a "disaster" when everyone is having fun.
- Games dissolve many learning problems.
- Learning is at its best when it is not being controlled by others!
- Games give meaning to abstract learning.
- Playing games builds memories that last a lifetime!
- To prevent failure...promote happiness in learning
- Parents who truly believe in themselves can relate this idea to their children.
- Be sensitive to the idea, "the world is as we construe it;" this shapes our behavior. How do you construe your child?
- We become what we think...
- What are you thinking about YOUR CHILD???

Chapter XII

What are you leading your child to think about "self"?? IT IS TIME TO PLAY! It is time for you and your child to begin the process of *Becoming...Whole.*

Agility - quickness; spryness; nimbleness of movement

Analysis - dividing a whole into parts; studying the parts

Attention - steady concentration; mental effort to attend

> **Visual** - holding attention to symbols seen
>
> **Auditory** - attending to sounds, etc., heard
>
> **Motor** - attending to motor activity
>
> **Spatial attention** - attending to spatial arrangement and place

Auditory Association - mentally dealing with auditory information received; dealing with analogies and responding verbally to missing parts of analogy

Auditory Closure - receiving parts of words auditorially and responding with the missing part

Auditory Discrimination - the distinguishing of different sounds, blends, words, noises, etc.; telling one sound from another; understanding the difference in things heard

Auditory Memory - remembering from hearing

Auditory Perception - understanding gained from sounds heard

Auditory Recall - remembering single or sequential items immediately

> **Immediate Recall** - current recall
>
> **Short term Recall** - remembering after an interruption
>
> **Long Term Recall** - remembering after two or more interruptions

Auditory Reception - includes the receiving of information heard, acting upon on it through analysis, synthesis or discrimination and responding

Auditory Sequential Memory - the received auditory information and reproduction of same through spoken language

GLOSSARY

Auditory Sound Blending - receives auditory information by hearing words through sounds, blends etc., synthesizing process puts these together for saying

Auditory vocabulary - words known from sound

Body Image - awareness of body, its relation to orientation, movement and other behavior

Comprehension - ability to understand things read, said or done

Compulsiveness - inability to move focus of attention from one small part to whole for learning

Conceptualization - inferring what is received visually, auditorially, or through any other of the senses

Conceptualizing - thinking, recognizing and internalizing relationships and ideas

Continual Process - going to the Mart; seeing all games on display;

THE SEARCH...NEVER ENDING...

Cross Modality - receiving information by one mode, putting it out through another; (Ex. seeing visually and saying orally)

Decoding - receptive language habits (e.g. sensory acuity, awareness, discrimination, vocabulary comprehension)

Directionality - awareness of the up and down axis and of side versus side of body (laterally)

Discrimination - seeing or hearing the differences in sounds, symbols

Encoding - expressive habits in language process; i.e. response formation including word selection, syntax, grammar and motor production of response

Eye Hand Coordination - where the eye guides the hand in writing and other coordinated movement

Eye Tracking - muscular movement of the eye; visually following an object; following lines in reading; an aid to visual motor integration

Figure Ground - Finding one part of a perceptual configuration to stand out while rest is background

Fine Motor - Ability to coordinate eye hand in fine movement; fine muscle movement

Gwen's Ideas -

1. that she was in charge...ever
2. that Todd would be a perfect playmate...(Gwen is smart.)
3. to write this book
4. to leave town to write now and then
5. to use bananas as paper weights at the River Park excursion Imagery - representation of images

Impulsivity - initiation of sudden action without sufficient forethought

I.R.S. - sixteenth amendment

Lateral Awareness - perceiving objects as being to the right or to left of self

Laterality - separation of the right sides of the body on motor level

Modality - an avenue of acquiring sensation; visual, auditory tactile, kinesthetic, olfactory and gustatory are common modalities

Motor Skills - pertaining to the origin or execution of muscular activity

Multisensory - applied to training procedures utilizing more than one sense modality, simultaneously

Patience - waiting...waiting...waiting...waiting...pleasantly!!!

Perception - recognition of quality without distinguishing meaning, the result of complex reactions includes sensory stimulation, organization, within the nervous system and memory; an immediate or intuitive judgement involving subtle discriminations

Personal List - personal lists are...personal; YOURS ONLY...

PLAYMATES - two people who play together constantly, comfortably; no stress; no anger...ever!

Reacting - (not same as calm response); active reply or retort; given in opposition, often

Recall - remembering items seen or sounds heard, bringing forth for user

Responding - saying or doing something in answer; thoughtful, controlled reply

Reversal - Incorrect spatial orientation of letters; incorrect order of letters in words

Self Concept - person's idea of self; feeling about the way he views self

Sequential Memory - immediate ordered recall (visual, auditory, motor, etc.,)

Short Term memory - immediate recall

Sight Vocabulary - words known visually Similarities - items somewhat alike

Sorting - distinguishing differences

Spatial - awareness of space around; distance, form, direction, position

Spiritual Growth - self is growing, accepting spirit within Strategy (authors definition)- a thought pattern that settles in the brain and becomes "a foundation for future learning"

Todd's ideas:

1. to teach Gwen Chess! (Todd's mistake!)

2. to teach Gwen to play Operation without a nervous breakdown

3. that strategies were the whole before the parts were located

4. origin of natural learning

5. to go to the mountains

6. to write at the River park; with pages flying in the wind

7. to take a pen and pad with us...wherever we are Um-mmph - all of your get up and go in one package

Visual Association - child receives information visually from pictures, selects slightly different picture and associates

Visual Closure - visual symbol information received, responds filling in missing parts

Visual Coordination - understanding symbols seen

Visual Discrimination - ability to identify, separate similarities and differences in visual forms

Visual Figure Ground - ability to locate form on distracting background

Visual Motor - relating visual stimuli to motor responses appropriately

Visual Motor Memory - remembering characteristics of forms seen visually with motor movement

Visual Perception - (see perception)

Visual Reception - child's ability to receive visual information from symbols; act upon it, analyze, synthesize or discriminate, respond

Visual Sequential Memory - reproduces visual forms seen in sequence within a time limit

Word Attack - using all skills of sounding and blending letters in the process of determining words

BIBLIOGRAPHY

Bolles, Richard Nelson, *What Color is Your Parachute?* Berkeley: Ten Speed Press, 1984.

Brown, Alan S., *Maximizing Memory Power.* New York: John Wiley and Sons, Inc., 1987.

DeBono, Edward, *New Think.* New York: Avon Books, 1971.

Engelmann, Siegfried and Therese, *Give Your Child a Superior Mind.* New York: Simon and Schuster, 1981.

Gazzaniga, Michael S., *The Social Brain: Discovering the Networks of the Mind.* New York: Basic Books, Inc., 1985.

Holt, John, *How Children Fail.* New York: Dell, 1982.

Holt, John, *How Children Learn.* New York: Dell, 1983.

McGuire, Jack, *What Does Childhood Taste Like?* New York: The Stonesong Press, 1986.

Ornstein, Robert and Richard F. Thompson, *The Amazing Brain.* Boston: Houghton Mifflin Company, 1986.

Osman, Betty B., *Learning Disabilities:* A Family Affair. New York: Warner Books, Inc., 1979.

Packard, Vance, *Our Endangered Children: Growing Up In a Changing World.* New York: Little, Brown and Company, 1983.

Peck, Scott M., *The Road Less Traveled.* New York: Simon and Schuster, 1978.

Powell, John, *Unconditional Love.* Allen,Texas: Argus, 1978.

Radar, Melvin, *The Enduring Questions: Main Problems of Philosophy.* New York: Holt, Rinehart and Wilson, 1980.

Rennold, Joyce and Helen Beard Corson, *The Energy Connection.* Atlanta: Rencor Publishing, 1986.

Restak, Richard M., *The Brain: The Last Frontier.* New York: Warner Books, 1979.

BIBLIOGRAPHY

Rosner, Jerome, *Helping Children Overcome Learning Difficulties.* New York: Walker and Company, 1979.

Segalowitz, Sid J., *Two Sides of the Brain.* New Jersey: Prentice Hall, Inc., 1983.

Sparling, Joseph and Isabelle Lewis, *Learning Games for the First Three Years.* New York: Walker and Company, 1984.

Springer, Sally and George Deutsch, *Left Brain, Right Brain.* New York: W.H. Freeman and Company, 1985.

Sutton-Smith, Brian and Shirley, *How To Play With Your Children.* New York: Hawthorn Dutton, 1974.

Vitale, Barbara Mesiter, *Unicorns Are Real:* A Right Brained Approach to Learning. California: Jalmar Press, 1982.

Wittig, Arno F., *Psychology of Learning.* New York: McGraw Hill, 1981.

A very special thank you for the research material so graciously shared with us from the:
Office of Educational Research and Improvement
United States Department of Education
Washington, D.C., 20208.

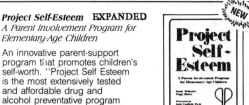

Learning The Skills of Peacemaking
An Activity Guide for Elementary-Age Children

"Global peace begins with you. Guide develops this fundamental concept in fifty lessons. If this curriculum was a required course in every elementary school in every country, we would see world peace in our children's lifetimes." — *Letty Cottin Pogrebin*, Ms. Magazine
0-915190-46-X $21.95
8½ × 11 paperback, illus.

Project Self-Esteem EXPANDED
A Parent Involvement Program for Elementary-Age Children

An innovative parent-support program that promotes children's self-worth. "Project Self Esteem is the most extensively tested and affordable drug and alcohol preventative program available."

0-915190-59-1 $39.95
8½ × 11 paperback, illus.

The Two Minute Lover
Announcing A New Idea In Loving Relationships

No one is foolish enough to imagine that s/he *automatically* deserves success. Yet, almost everyone thinks that they automatically deserve sudden and continuous success in marriage. Here's a book that helps make that belief a reality.
0-915190-52-4 $9.95
6 × 9 paperback, illus.

Reading, Writing and Rage

An autopsy of one profound school failure, disclosing the complex processes behind it and the secret rage that grew out of it.

Must reading for anyone working with learning disabled, functional illiterates, or juvenile delinquents.

0-915190-42-7 $16.95
5½ × 8½ paperback

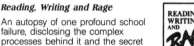

Feel Better Now
30 Ways to Handle Frustration in Three Minutes or Less

Most of us realize that letting go of tension is a key to happiness and health. This book explains the dynamics of letting go.

0-915190-66-4 $9.95
6 X 9 paperback

Esteem Builders

You CAN improve your students' behavior and achievement through building self-esteem. Here is a book packed with classroom- proven techniques, activities, and ideas you can immediately use in your own program or at home.

Ideas, ideas, ideas, for grades K-8 and parents.

0-915190-53-2 $39.95
8½ × 11 paperback, illus.

Good Morning Class—I Love You!
Thoughts and Questions About Teaching from the Heart

A book that helps create the possibility of having schools be places where students, teachers and principals get what every human being wants and needs—LOVE!

0-915190-58-3 $6.95
5½ × 8½ paperback, illus.

I am a blade of grass
A Breakthrough in Learning and Self-Esteem

Help your students become "lifetime learners," empowered with the confidence to make a positive difference in their world (without abandoning discipline or sacrificing essential skill and content acquisition).
0-915190-54-0 $14.95
6 × 9   paperback, illus.

Unlocking Doors to Self-Esteem

Presents innovative ideas to make the secondary classroom a more positive learning experience—socially and emotionally—for students and teachers. Over 100 lesson plans included. Designed for easy infusion into curriculum. Gr. 7-12

0-915190-60-5 $16.95
6 × 9 paperback, illus

SAGE: *Self-Awareness Growth Experiences*

A veritable treasure trove of activities and strategies promoting positive behavior and meeting the personal/ social needs of young people in grades 7-12. Organized around affective learning goals and objectives. Over 150 activities.
0-915190-61-3 $16.95
6 × 9 paperback, illus.

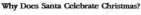

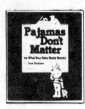

Pajamas Don't Matter:
(or What Your Baby Really Needs)

Here's help for new parents every-where! Provides valuable information and needed reassurances to new parents as they struggle through the frantic, but rewarding, first years of their child's life.
0-915190-21-4 $5.95
8½ x 11   paperback, full color

Why Does Santa Celebrate Christmas?

What do wisemen, shepherds and angels have to do with Santa, reindeer and elves? Explore this Christmas fantasy which ties all of the traditions of Christmas into one lovely poem for children of all ages.
0-915190-67-2 $12.95
8 1/2 x 11 hardcover, full color

Feelings Alphabet

Brand-new kind of alphabet book full of photos and word graphics that will delight readers of all ages."...lively, candid...the 26 words of this pleasant book express experiences common to all children." *Library Journal*
0-935266-15-1 $7.95
6 x 9   paperback, B/W photos

The Parent Book

A functional and sensitive guide for parents who want to enjoy every min-ute of their child's growing years. Shows how to live with children in ways that encourage healthy emo-tional development. Ages 3-14.
0-915190-15-X $9.95
8½ x 11   paperback, illus.

Aliens In My Nest
SQUIB Meets The Teen Creature

Squib comes home from summer camp to find that his older brother, Andrew, has turned into a snarly, surly, defiant, and non-communica-tive adolescent. *Aliens* explores the effect of Andrew's new behavior on Squib and the entire family unit.
0-915190-49-4 $7.95
8½ x 11   paperback, illus.

Hugs & Shrugs
The Continuing Saga of SQUIB

Squib feels incomplete. He has lost a piece of himself. He searches every where only to discover that his miss-ing piece has fallen in and not out. He becomes complete again once he discovers his own inner-peace.

0-915190-47-8 $7.95
8½ x 11   paperback, illus.

Moths & Mothers/
Feather & Fathers
A Story About a Tiny Owl Named SQUIB

Squib is a tiny owl who cannot fly. Neither can he understand his feel-ings. He must face the frustration, grief, fear, guilt and loneliness that we all must face at different times in our lives. Struggling with these feel-ings, he searches, at least, for understanding.

0-915190-57-5 $7.95
8½ x 11   paperback, illus.

Hoots & Toots & Hairy Brutes
The Continuing Adventures of SQUIB

Squib—who can only toot—sets out to learn how to give a mighty hoot. His attempts result in abject failure. Every reader who has struggled with life's limitations will recognize their own struggles and triumphs in the microcosm of Squib's forest world. A parable for all ages from 8 to 80.

0-915190-56-7 $7.95
8½ x 11   paperback, illus.

Do I Have To Go To School Today?
Squib Measures Up!

Squib dreads the daily task of going to school. In this volume, he daydreams about all the reasons he has not to go. But, in the end, Squib convinces himself to go to school because his teacher accepts him "Just as he is!"

0-915190-62-1 $7.95
8½ x 11   paperback, illus.

The Turbulent Teens
Understanding Helping Surviving

"This book should be read by every parent of a teenager in America...It gives a parent the information needed to understand teenagers and guide them wisely."—Dr. Fitzhugh Dodson, author of *How to Parent, How to Father, and How to Discipline with Love.*
0-913091-01-4 $8.95
6 x 9   paperback.

Openmind/Wholemind
Parenting & Teaching Tomorrow's Children Today

A book of powerful possibilities that honors the capacities, capabilities, and potentials of adult and child alike. Uses Modalities, Intelligences, Styles and Creativity to explore how the brain-mind system acquires, processes and expresses experience. Foreword by M. McClaren & C. Charles.
0-915190-45-1 $14.95
7 × 9 paperback
81 B/W photos   29 illus.

Present Yourself! *Captivate Your Audience With Great Presentation Skills*

Become a presenter who is a dynamic part of the message. Learn about Transforming Fear, Knowing Your Audience, Setting The Stage, Making Them Remember and much more. Essential reading for anyone interested in the art of communication. Destined to become the standard work in its field.
0-915190-51-6 paper $9.95
0-915190-50-8 cloth $18.95
6 × 9 paper/cloth. illus.

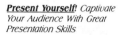

Unicorns Are Real
A Right-Brained Approach to Learning

Over 100,000 sold. The long-awaited "right hemispheric" teaching strategies developed by popular educational specialist Barbara Vitale are now available. Hemispheric dominance screening instrument included.
0-915190-35-4 $12.95
8½ × 11 paperback, illus.

Unicorns Are Real Poster

Beautifully-illustrated. Guaranteed to capture the fancy of young and old alike. Perfect gift for unicorn lovers, right-brained thinkers and all those who know how to dream. For classroom, office or home display.

JP9027 $4.95
19 × 27 full color

Imagination is the unicorn that lifts us above the mundane chains that bind the minds of many and flies us on fantastic wings to a place where dreams DO come true.

Practical Application, Right Hemisphere Learning Methods

Audio from Barbara Vitale. Discover many practical ways to successfully teach right-brained students using whole-to-part learning, visualization activities, color stimuli, motor skill techniques and more.
JP9110 $12.95
Audio Cassette

Don't Push Me, I'm Learning as Fast as I Can

Barbara Vitale presents some remarkable insights on the physical growth stages of children and how these stages affect a child's ability, not only to learn, but to function in the classroom.
JP9112 $12.95
Audio Cassette

Metaphoric Mind (Revised Ed.)

Here is a plea for a balanced way of thinking and being in a culture that stands on the knife-edge between catastrophe and transformation. The metaphoric mind is asking again, quietly but insistently, for equilibrium. For, after all, equilibrium is the way of nature.
0-915190-68-0 $14.95
7 x 10 paperback, B/W photos

Free Flight *Celebrating Your Right Brain*

Journey with Barbara Vitale, from her uncertain childhood perceptions of being "different" to the acceptance and adult celebration of that difference. A book for right-brained people in a left-brained world. Foreword by Bob Samples.
0-915190-44-3 $9.95
5½ × 8½ paperback, illus.

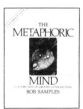

"He Hit Me Back First"
Self-Esteem through Self-Discipline

Simple techniques for guiding children toward self-correcting behavior as they become aware of choice and their own inner authority.
0-915190-36-2   **$12.95**
8½ × 11 paperback, illus.

Learning To Live, Learning To Love

An inspirational message about the importance of love in everything we do. Beautifully told through words and pictures. Ageless and timeless.
0-915190-38-9 $7.95
6 × 9 paperback, illus.

TA For Tots
(and other prinzes)
Over 500,000 sold.

This innovative book has helped thousands of young children and their parents to better understand and relate to each other. Ages 4-9.
0-915190-12-5 $12.95
8½ × 11 paper, color, illus.

TA For Tots, Vol. II
Explores new ranges of feelings and suggests solutions to problems such as feeling hurt, sad, shy, greedy, or lonely.
Ages 4-9.
0-915190-25-7 $12.95
8½ × 11 paper, color, illus.

TA For Tots Coloring Book
Constructive, creative coloring fun! The charming *TA For Tots* characters help show kids that taking care of their feelings is OK! Ages 2-9.
0-915190-33-8 $1.95
8½·× 11 saddle stitched, illus.

TA Today I'm OK Poster
Cheerful, happy TA creatures help convey the most positive, upbeat message to be found. Perfect for brightening your room or office.
JP9002 $3.00
19 × 27 full color poster

TA for Kids
(and grown-ups too)
Over 250,000 sold.

The message of TA is presented in simple, clear terms so youngsters can apply it in their daily lives. Warm Fuzzies abound. Ages 9-13.
0-915190-09-5 $9.95
8½ × 11 paper, color, illus.

TA For Teens
(and other important people)
Over 100,000 sold.

Using the concepts of Transactional Analysis. Dr. Freed explains the ups and downs of adulthood without talking down to teens. Ages 13-18.
0-915190-03-6 $18.95
8½ × 11 paperback, illus.

Original Warm Fuzzy Tale
Learn about "Warm Fuzzies" firsthand.
Over 100,000 sold.

A classic fairytale...with adventure, fantasy, heroes, villains and a moral. Children (and adults, too) will enjoy this beautifully illustrated book.
0-915190-08-7 $7.95
6 × 9 paper, full color, illus.

Songs of The Warm Fuzzy
"All About Your Feelings"
The album includes such songs as Hitting is Harmful, Being Scared, When I'm Angry, Warm Fuzzy Song, Why Don't Parents Say What They Mean, and I'm Not Perfect (Nobody's Perfect).
JP9003R/C $12.95
Cassette

Tot Pac *(Audio-Visual Kit)*
Includes 5 filmstrips, 5 cassettes, 2 record LP album. A *Warm Fuzzy I'm OK* poster, 8 coloring posters, 10 Warm Fuzzies. 1 *TA for Tots* and 92 page *Leader's Manual*. No prior TA training necessary to use Tot Pac in the classroom! Ages 2-9.
JP9032 $150.00
Multimedia program

Kid Pac *(Audio-Visual Kit)*
Teachers, counselors, and parents of pre-teens will value this easy to use program. Each *Kid Pac* contains 13 cassettes, 13 filmstrips, 1 *TA For Kids*, and a comprehensive *Teacher's Guide*, plus 10 Warm Fuzzies. Ages 9-13.
JP9033 $195.00
Multimedia Program